TWENTY CHOICES TO ABUNDANT LIFE

A medical doctor's perspective on the fullness of the Christian life

ROBERT F ARROM MD

ENDORSEMENTS

"With stories, Scripture, and deep insight, *Twenty Choices to Abundant Life* shares principles that can change your life and the life of those you love. Well worth your read!"

David Stevens, MD, MA (Ethics)
Chief Executive Officer, Christian Medical & Dental Association

"Dr. Robert Arrom, a gifted physician and medical missionary, provides the reader with a fascinating account of his many medical missionary ventures, intertwined with biblical truths about finding true joy and purpose in life. By making right choices we live abundant lives, as Dr. Arrom clearly and convincingly argues. This book will appeal to believers searching for deeper insights into purposeful and authentic Christian living, and to seekers who wonder how to achieve true happiness in this life."

Robert J. Lerer, MD, FAAP
Chairman of the Board, Caring Partners International
Associate Professor of Pediatrics, The University of Cincinnati College of Medicine
Commissioner of Health, Butler County, Ohio, USA

"This book is a glimpse into the heart of a true missionary. Those of us who have the pleasure of sharing in professional service with Dr. Robert Arrom know him to be a person of great devotion, passion, and compassion who gives loving service within our community as well as to some of the most remote and deprived civilizations of the world. This book clearly directs us to the inspiration for his life and his vocation, his experience of God's love in Christ. I commend this book to you with the prayer that it may encourage us all to a more devoted Christian life and selfless service."

Stan Dunk, MDiv, BCC
Director of Pastoral Care, Fort Hamilton Hospital

TWENTY CHOICES TO ABUNDANT LIFE

A medical doctor's perspective on the fullness of the Christian life

ROBERT F ARROM MD

Copyright © 2011 Robert F Arrom MD

All rights reserved.

ISBN: 1456527347
ISBN-13: 9781456527341

All Scripture quotations, unless otherwise indicated, are taken from the *HOLY BIBLE, NEW INTERNATIONAL VERSION®. NIV®.* Copyright © 1973, 1978, 1984 International Bible Society. Used by permission of Zondervan. All rights reserved.

Scriptures marked KJV are from the King James Version of the Bible.

DEDICATION

To Carol Arrom, RN

My wife, best friend, soul mate, and companion,
My partner in life and in missions,
My true love, who exemplifies many of the Christian virtues portrayed here.
To her this book is dedicated.

CONTENTS

Foreword by Dr. Harold Graves .... **xi**
Acknowledgments .... **xiii**
Introduction .... **xv**

1. Choose Light over Darkness 1
2. Choose Love over Hate 11
3. Choose Serving over Being Served 19
4. Choose Hope over Despair 27
5. Choose Joy over Sadness 35
6. Choose Holiness over Worldliness 43
7. Choose Faith over Doubt 53
8. Choose Giving over Receiving 61
9. Choose Strength over Weakness 69
10. Choose Life over Death 79
11. Choose Peace over Strife 87
12. Choose Courage over Fear 97
13. Choose Thankfulness over Anger 109
14. Choose Being Healed over Being Sick 115
15. Choose Wisdom over Foolishness 121
16. Choose Forgiveness over Unforgiveness 129
17. Choose Honesty over Dishonesty 137
18. Choose Making a Difference over Being Indifferent 145
19. Choose Justice over Injustice 153
20. Choose Having a Vision over Having No Vision 165
21. What Shall I Take for the Journey? 173

Epilogue **181**
About the Author **183**

FOREWORD

We live in a world filled with challenges, surprises, and opportunities. We do not need to be reminded of the perilous times we are living in. The present economic malaise has created a tsunami of financial erosion that has undermined even the strongest of institutions. Recent events have challenged the most conventional of Judeo-Christian values and beliefs. Many have suggested that the United States is shifting into a post-Christendom phase.

In view of the seismic shifts in the culture and the tenuous state of the economy, Dr. Bob Arrom gives personal witness to a life of faith, hope, and love. In *Twenty Choices to Abundant Life,* he shares essential truths about the Christian faith. He writes from a life of experience as an exceptional physician, committed follower of Christ, and dedicated husband and father.

Written to encourage those who have lost their joy and hope, this book combines Scripture insights and personal stories of faith to inspire and enrich the reader.

I have known Bob for several years and have witnessed his growth in the Lord and his love for people. Bob's desire to share his faith story and lead others into the abundant life is the inspiration for this book.

I recommend *Twenty Choices to Abundant Life* as a book that will lift your hearts and set your sights on a new way of living and giving.

Dr. Harold B. Graves, Jr., President
Nazarene Bible College

ACKNOWLEDGMENTS

The author wishes to thank the following persons for their contributions to this book:

1. Dr. Harold Graves, Jr., friend and former pastor, president of the Nazarene Bible College in Colorado Springs, Colorado, for his review of the manuscript for theological accuracy and content, and for writing the Foreword.
2. Carol Ann Arrom, RN, the one who shares my burdens, my wife and fellow missionary, for her review and critique of the manuscript.
3. Dennis Eliasen, friend and brother in Christ, for his review and critique of the manuscript.
4. Jerry Heatherly, pastor and friend, for his review of the manuscript and his encouragement.
5. Robert J. Lerer, MD, friend, fellow missionary, and brother in Christ, for his review and critique of the manuscript, and for his lifelong friendship.
6. Christopher Brown, friend and fellow Christian brother, for his expert review of the early manuscript and constructive criticism.
7. Kimberly Couch, coworker at my medical office, for typing the original manuscript and enduring with grace and patience the necessary corrections.
8. Karen Roberts, friend and fellow Christian, for her critique of the manuscript and able editorial advice.

Without the help, love, and encouragement of these people, this book would not be a reality. To them I owe a debt of gratitude that I can never repay.

Robert Arrom, MD

INTRODUCTION

We are all made for greatness. The seeds of greatness are planted in our souls when the breath of life is breathed into our nostrils. We are made in the image of the invisible God, and we have received the potential to live a life that is abundant.

We are children of the light, born of God, meant to do great things, but we are also made of clay, of molded earth, with the seeds of our own destruction also planted into our being.

The path that we take in life depends on the choices we make. Throughout our lifetime we will face many difficulties and challenges. Our success or failure will depend upon our foundations and the choices that we make.

The path that leads to greatness and abundant life is the road less traveled, the one that seems harder to trod, and the one that seems counterintuitive and countercultural. It is the one that is opposite to the wisdom of the world, which suggests that happiness lies in the pursuit of riches and possessions. To be great is to be small and humble, not the ruler but the servant, the one who has all because he has given all.

Abundant life is a life of spiritual richness and productivity, of fruitfulness and obedience. It is the reward of those who know God and seek Him with all their hearts. It is the reward of those who know the voice of the Shepherd and follow exactly what He commands—without compromise, exceptions, or regrets.

Abundant life is a state of unique identity and oneness with our Creator. It is a preview of what is to come, a window into eternal life.

Abundant life is not a life free from worry or worldly concerns, or free from troubles or tribulation. It is not about money. It is a state of being well equipped and adequately suited to meet the challenges that lay ahead in the knowledge that God is in control of all things, and that with God all things are possible. It is confidence in God's plan for our lives. It means to depend on Him and not on our own ability or our own understanding.

Abundant life means to enjoy the riches of God, knowing that we are forgiven when we sincerely repent of our sins, and that we can share in God's promises and in God's glory. When we are living the abundant life, we can look trouble in the eye and not be afraid, knowing that nothing can separate us from the love of God: not sickness or death, not financial downturns or natural disasters. God is with us and in us, and He will never leave us.

We can say with confidence, as the prophet Isaiah wrote, that God is with us in every circumstance, as He promised: "When you pass through the waters, I will be with you; and when you pass through the rivers, they will not sweep over you. When you walk through the fire, you will not be burned; the flames will not set you ablaze" (Isaiah 43:2).

Most importantly, abundant life is the promise and the reward of those who search for the Lord with all their hearts. Jesus said, "I am come that they might have life, and that they might have it more abundantly" (John 10:10 KJV).

It is my sincere wish and desire that all who read these pages will find true greatness in the service of others. May they receive life abundant here on earth and, thereafter, have eternal life. It is my hope that in each chapter the Spirit of God is evident, despite my modest abilities and understanding of things eternal.

This book is an offering of love to my fellow workers in the vineyard of the Lord: to those fellow travelers in the journey of life who search for the truth and, having found it, cannot wait to tell others. As an evangelist once said, "I too am just a hungry man telling another where he found bread." May it be to God's glory!

CHAPTER 1
CHOOSE LIGHT OVER DARKNESS

Most of us receive citizenship in a country by the mere act of being born there. It is completely effortless on our part, and it is automatically given; yet it represents a great gift.

For others, citizenship requires an elaborate and formal ceremony where a group of applicants gather before a judge. Each applicant must have met all the requirements of the law, including time of legal residence in the country, demonstrated respect for the law by having passed a background check, and a passing grade on a history and citizenship test. The venue is decorated with the flags of the native countries of the applicants gathered for the ceremony, as well as the flag of their newly adopted land. With great devotion and fervor, they recite the oath of citizenship. Often it is an emotional and tearful ceremony. From that moment on, they are citizens of their new country, with all the rights and responsibilities of citizenship.

Far more important than our earthly citizenship is the establishment of our citizenship in the kingdom of heaven. To do so, we do not need to have met all the requirements of the Law or to have lived a perfect life, but simply to accept Jesus as our Lord and Savior. "Everyone who calls on the name of the Lord will be saved" (Romans 10:13).

Of all the choices we must make in life, perhaps this one is the most important and the most fundamental. We must decide once and for all where our spiritual citizenship is. It is a simple truth that where our loyalties and treasures are also is where our spirit is at home. We must decide to whom we belong. If we belong to the Lord, our citizenship is in heaven, and we are children of the Light. If we do not choose the Light, we belong to the darkness.

We do not have two spirits. We cannot be both holy, live in the light, and at the same time live in darkness, prisoners of the flesh and of our sinful nature. Simply stated, we cannot sit both at the Lord's Table and at the table of the Devil. We must choose where our spirit calls its home and let our spirit dwell there.

Declaring Our Citizenship

We declare our spiritual citizenship by accepting Jesus into our hearts. In doing so, we renounce our sinful nature and become temples of the Holy Spirit, "to offer your bodies as living sacrifices to God" (Romans 12:1). God responds to our heartfelt choice immediately by commissioning us as bearers of the light, and we receive "the fruit of the Spirit ... love, joy, peace, patience, kindness, goodness, faithfulness, gentleness and self-control (Galatians 5:22–23).

Once we declare our spiritual citizenship in heaven, we become children of the Light, and our lives radiate the Light of God over the darkness of the world. As children of the Light, we delight in the law of the Lord, and in that law we meditate day and night (see Psalm 1:2). Our thoughts turn from evil and are filled with goodness.

If we live by the Spirit, surrendering to His will over ours, we will not satisfy the desires of our sinful nature. "The sinful nature desires what is contrary to the spirit" (Galatians 5:17). But if we choose not to surrender completely, we grieve the Holy Spirit and allow room in our lives for "the acts of the sinful nature ... sexual immorality, impurity and debauchery; idolatry and witchcraft; hatred, discord, jealousy, fits of rage, selfish ambition, dissensions, fractions and envy, drunkenness, orgies, and the like" (Galatians 5:19–21).

Living in the Light

Living in the Light requires conscious choices. These, then, are what we must choose to do for the Light to shine brightly in us:

1. <u>Daily devotions</u>: spend time learning and knowing the word of God, meditating upon and memorizing Scripture until it becomes engraved in our hearts. "The sword of the Spirit, which is the word of God" (Ephesians 6:17), is our only defensive weapon in the armor of God (see Ephesians 6:11).
2. <u>Daily prayer</u>: pray continuously and under all circumstances. Strive to maintain an ongoing conversation with God. Prayer is essential in order to overcome temptation ("pray so that you will not fall into temptation," Matthew 26:41), leaning not on our own power, for we are weak, but leaning on God's power and strength.
3. <u>Godly actions</u>: reflect our citizenship in the kingdom of heaven by our daily actions. Our salvation must be evident to all in all we do. The Light is reflected in our dress, our behavior, and our words. We must strive, therefore, to have complete control of our tongues and our bodies.
4. <u>Love</u>: demonstrate God's love to others. Our love must be evident to all. We must choose to love God with all of our hearts and follow the Golden Rule: love our neighbors as ourselves. They will know that we are Christians by our love ("by this all men will know that you are my disciples, if you love one another," John 13:35). But we must also love those who do not love us, those who persecute us and those who offend us (see Matthew 5:44–47). Perhaps this teaching is one of the most difficult ones of the gospel, but it is one that must be observed and practiced. It requires forgiveness of those who hurt us, insult us, and falsely accuse us. If we cannot forgive, neither will we be forgiven.
5. <u>Works</u>: have works that reflect our salvation and our status as citizens of the kingdom of heaven and children of the Light. It is true that we are saved by faith and not by works, so no one can boast (see Ephesians 2:8–9). It is also true that "as the body without the spirit is dead, so faith without deeds is dead" (James 2:26). Our works, then, reflect our salvation and are tangible proofs of that salvation. We must embark on acts of kindness

and compassion described by our Lord: to feed those who have nothing to eat, give a drink of clean water in His name, care for those who are sick, visit those who are imprisoned, and clothe those that have nothing to wear (see Mathew 25).
6. <u>Partnership with others</u>: partner with Christian relief organizations and participate in their work at home and overseas. We must support organizations that look after those who are less fortunate than we are with our prayers and our time, with our money and our talents. We must also protect life and defend the unborn.

These last two points deserve special attention. Many of us can actually go overseas to help feed the hungry masses; to help care for the orphans and widows of the HIV/AIDS epidemic in Africa; or to help restore the lives of the victims of wars, epidemics, or natural disasters. Opportunities abound. Regrettably, few are the workers in the vineyards of the Lord. It is therefore imperative that we translate our faith into action and into works that glorify God. In so doing, we pass our light on to others so that the Light will never be extinguished.

Light Transforms Darkness

The world has seldom seen as dark a time as the Jewish Holocaust during the Second World War. The persecution of the Jewish people—their deportation to concentration camps in cattle trains and their extermination in the most cruel and inhumane ways, which included gas chambers, the hanging of children, and the cremation of live people—are beyond description and have left a dark stain in history. Yet out of the smoldering ashes of the Holocaust emerged Eli Wiesel, a survivor of the concentration camps and an eloquent witness to the suffering of the Jewish people. In his book, *Night* (Bantam Books, 1982), he portrays the numerous indignities, humiliations, and horrors inflicted upon six million people. These acts of immense cruelty were perpetrated for the most part by educated people, while other educated people watched in silence.

"Never shall I forget the little faces of the children, whose bodies I saw turned into wreaths of smoke beneath the silent blue sky. Never shall I forget the nocturnal silence which deprived me for all eternity of the desire to live," says Wiesel (32). His book is appropriately titled *Night* because it truly reflects one of the darkest chapters in human history.

Eli Wiesel is not only a survivor of the Holocaust. He is a bright light for one of the darkest nights of the human soul. He was able to renew his faith in God after having lost it. He was also able to believe in the basic goodness of all human beings despite his personal experience with the darkness. For his work he was granted the 1986 Nobel Peace Prize.

Our light often shines brightest in the darkest night: the deeper the darkness, the brighter the light.

The Light of Missions

In stark contrast with the darkness of our times (where terrorism, wars, outbursts of violence, and mass murders are prevalent) stands the light of the church of Jesus Christ. Missions and missionaries are expressions of this light.

Because only one third of the world's 6.7 billion people are Christians (David Shibley, *The Missions Addiction* [Charisma House, 2001], 14), missions seek to transform lives by bringing the good news of the gospel to the 1.6 billion people who have not heard it (in some cases as well as to the 2 billion who have heard but rejected it). Missions are about the sowing of seeds that contain the truth, the way, and the life that is in Jesus Christ and the harvest that follows.

The heart of missions is the transformation that takes place in people at the great encounter of the human soul with the Prince of Peace. Often the first person to undergo transformation is the missionary, or the one sent. He or she must undergo intense transformation in order to reflect the light of God, for even a good message may go unheard if the messenger is flawed.

All Christians, as children of the Light, are called to be missionaries of Jesus Christ. All must be His ambassadors and representatives. "You are the light of the world," Jesus told His followers (Matthew 5:14). We are all bearers of the light; we are all transformed people because of our repentance and the forgiveness of our sins.

Missions are also about meeting basic human needs. These needs include shelter, food, clean water, and health services; yet none are more important than the need to love and be loved and the need to know God. Each of us has a mission field. Our mission field is the person next to us who is tired, burdened, and desperate to hear the good news of the gospel. It is the people in our own homes and neighborhoods, in our city and our country; it is also those in foreign countries and faraway lands where some of us are called to serve.

Bearing the Light in Papua New Guinea

In the South Pacific Ocean, perched in the eastern part of the island of New Guinea, is the country of Papua New Guinea. It is a country of great natural beauty, with sandy beaches where turquoise waters wash and wane. Where rivers careen down steep waterfalls, and where dense fog and misty air fill the valleys. Papua New Guinea is the overseas place where my wife and I have been called to serve.

Mainland Papua New Guinea comprises 85 percent of the national territory, while the remaining 15 percent is made up of six hundred other islands. East of the mainland is the Bismarck Archipelago. Farther south is the long and narrow New Ireland. Westward are East and West New Britain, while Buka and Bougainville border in the east with the Salomon Islands. Most mainland inhabitants are ethnically Melanesian, while in the eastern islands they are of Micronesian and Polynesian origin.

Papua New Guinea is unique among the countries of the world in that its rugged geography forced its people to live in near complete isolation. As such, they did not benefit from the metallurgical advances of the Bronze Age but continued to use stone instruments until the first contact with Europeans. By reasons of geography, villages and towns not distant from each other grew distinct and separate. This separation allowed for the development of 850 different languages that are not linguistically related to each other. Out of the world's 6,000 languages, nearly one of every six originated there. Many tribes and groups remained isolated from the rest of the world until the 1930s, when the people of the Highlands first made contact with Europeans.

At first, when we traveled there with short-term missions teams, my wife and I thought of ourselves as guest workers or volunteers. As time went on, their plight, their sorrows, and their suffering became ours. We now feel their pain and share their burdens. We consider ourselves honorary citizens of that country. In their Tak Pidgin language, Papua New Guinea is now "ples bilong us" (our country).

In the Western Highlands Province, in the village of Kudjip, is where the Nazarene Hospital is located. There, nights are illuminated only by stars, and in the distance, one can hear the rhythmic tunes of drums. I recall a night in which the serene tranquility of the village was broken by loud voices bursting into the hospital's emergency room. There had been an accident down the road, and the four-bed area was soon crowded with the injured.

The five missionary physicians who worked at the hospital rushed into the ER. They were barely able to cope with the sudden influx of patients. Among them was a young child, no older than one year, who had been sick for a week. His mother had brought him in. Her loud screams were lost in the midst of the confusion. The young patient had just breathed his last breath.

One of the missionary physicians, Dr. Bill McCoy, and a visiting registered nurse from the United States, my wife, worked at resuscitating the young child. The "code blue" went on for fifteen minutes. All efforts were futile. He was too far gone. The missionary physician handed the child back to his mother and embraced them both. "Mama, me sorry," he said.

At that moment, the doctor and nurse were like Jesus, comforting the young mother. They advanced the kingdom of God by shining His light into the suffering world.

Choosing light over darkness is the most fundamental choice for living the abundant life God has made available to us. When we do so, we are transformed, and we become bearers of the light that is in Jesus Christ. We can then transform the world, shining light into the darkness—not by our power but by the power of Him who lives in us.

CHAPTER 2
CHOOSE LOVE OVER HATE

The two brothers grew up together but lived very different lives. Not surprisingly, they developed disparate worldviews and passionately held opposing political opinions, which deeply divided their family.

One was a successful medical doctor, a gifted surgeon, and role model whose life was an example of devotion and sacrifice. He was punished for speaking out against the injustices of the Communist regime of his native Cuba and for his decision to emigrate. The regime thought of him as a valuable asset and handed him an exemplary punishment. He was subjected to ostracism, isolation, and the confiscation of his properties. He was given a sentence, which he served, and was later allowed to leave Cuba. He first arrived in Spain and subsequently applied for and received political asylum in the United States.

This brother settled down in Miami, Florida, along with many other Cuban political refugees. He reestablished his medical practice and once again became hugely successful. Despite his success, he never forgot the injustices to which he had been subjected. For the rest of his life, he was filled with hatred for the Communist regime and became bitter toward it. He despised anyone that approved of or sympathized with it.

The other brother, the older of the two, was equally successful, having lived in the United States since the 1940s. He was an accomplished scholar and a full-time Spanish literature professor at the prestigious Yale University in New Haven, Connecticut. He held more liberal political views than his younger brother about the Communist regime in Cuba and believed in engagement of the regime as the best means to enact change. As such, he was a frequent Cuban government guest at Havana University, where he lectured on Cuban literature. He was well regarded as an international authority in Spanish literature and received during his lifetime many honorary degrees from different institutions, including Havana University.

The two brothers did not see eye to eye. They passionately held conflicting political views that eventually translated into outright hatred for each other. They finally stopped speaking to each other and had no further contact for more than thirty years. Their animosity divided the family into two separate groups that did not interact with each other either. Even though the brothers were reconciled toward the end of their lives, the legacy of decades of bitterness was hard to undo; their relationship remained lukewarm until they died. They were my uncles.

Some people believe it is possible to be followers of Jesus Christ and at the same time hate those who have hurt them. Some believe it is okay to hold a grudge if it is justified. The gospel, however, clearly tells us do to quite the opposite: to love those who have hurt us, to love our enemies and those who persecute us, and to forgive them all for their wrongdoings. We are to choose love over hate regardless of the circumstances.

The Civil Rights Movement

The American civil rights movement of the 1960s is a perfect example of this principle. This movement illustrates not only how difficult it can be sometimes to apply the principle of love over hate but also how important and transcendental it is to do so. Throughout a large part of American history, African Americans were victims of segregation and discrimination. They were treated as inferior beings. Their humanity was denied, and they were subjected to untold humiliations, beatings, lynching, and even murders, which for the most part went unpunished. They were not only denied their human rights but also their civil rights, manifested in their inability to vote and participate in the political discourse as well as their rejection from jobs, public transportation, restaurants, and centers of higher learning.

While it would seem natural under those circumstances to return hate for hate or violence for violence, to do so would only aggravate and escalate the problem. Hatred and violence polarize people, placing them further apart. Love unites people, bringing them closer together.

Slain civil rights leader Dr. Martin Luther King, Jr., is praised and remembered for having chosen peace over violence, love over hate. A memorable quotation explains his philosophy: "Darkness cannot drive out darkness, only light can do that. Hate cannot drive out hate, only love can do that" (*Strength to Love* [Augsburg Fortress, 1963], 47). Dr. King rightly connected love to light and darkness to hate. There is immense wisdom in his words, which have their roots in the gospel of Jesus Christ.

Dr. King's contribution to a peaceful resolution of the civil rights movement cannot be overstated. His strategy of nonviolent resistance emulated the successful approach advanced by Mohandas K. Gandhi in India during the 1940s that led to that country's independence from Great Britain. King's was not the only voice at the time. There were competing philosophies that included violent confrontation (such as the "Black Power" movement of Stokely Carmichael). In many American cities, there were riots and much talk of violence. In spite of the opposition to a peaceful solution, Dr. King prevailed in keeping the struggle for the freedom of the black man in America from requiring the death of white people.

The inescapable conclusion of the two examples above is that there is an enormous personal and spiritual price to pay for allowing hate into our hearts. It is clear that hate is capable of the destruction of a person, a family, and even a country.

In contrast to the way of hatred is the way of love. Love builds up, while hate tears down. Love begets more love, while hate begets more hate. Love propagates itself; regrettably, so does hate.

The Power of Hate

Hate is destructive to our moral fabric, leading to bitterness, the desire for revenge, hate-filled actions, and violence. Hate separates us from God and is, therefore, a sin. "Anyone who claims to be in the light but hates his brother is still in the darkness" (1 John 2:9). God is love (see 1 John 4:8), and in Him there is no hate. Neither should we harbor hate in our hearts, for it destroys the soul.

Examples of hate abound in modern history: apartheid, segregation, the Ku Klux Klan, Nazism, anti-Semitism; racism in all its forms; discrimination against ethnic groups, such as Italians, Irish, and Hispanics; and the present discrimination against Muslims and homosexuals.

The teaching and practice of hate leads to damnation; it is unspiritual, unholy, and of the Devil. "Anyone who hates his brother is a murderer, and you know that no murderer has eternal life" (1 John 3:15). We must beware of those who sponsor the way of hatred. In them there is darkness: no truth, no light. The choice to follow the path of hate leads to death of the soul, but the choice to follow the gospel of love leads to peace and eternal life.

The Power of Love

Fortunately examples of love abound in our world as well: Christian missions, the Salvation Army, World Vision, Nazarene Compassionate Ministries, Catholic Charities, and Shared Harvest, to name just a few.

Love is God's idea. God is love, and He is the source of all love. His love goes beyond life and death, and it transcends all understanding. John 3:16 states the extent of His love clearly: "for God so loved the world that he gave his one and only Son, that whoever believes in him shall not perish but have eternal life." It is perplexing and truly amazing that God should love us because, as sinners and members of a fallen race, we have not always loved Him; it is even more amazing that He should die for us.

God's love is our example and our inspiration for how to love Him and others. In return for the undeserved love we have received from Him, we are to give to others some of what God has given us. Because He loved us first, we can love others, "for Christ's love compels us" (2 Corinthians 5:14).

Love in Action

One of the most beautiful statements ever written about love is recorded in 1 Corinthians 13. It states that no matter what qualification, gifts, talents, or virtues we may have, if we do not have love, we have nothing. It also says, "Love is patient, love is kind. It does not envy, it does not boast, it is not proud. It is not rude, it is not self-seeking, it is not easily angered, and it keeps no record of wrongs. Love does not delight in evil but rejoices with the truth" (1 Corinthians 13: 4–6).

In other words, love is not about us, but about others. It is about being humble, small, having a little rather than a large ego, being kind. This way of living is definitely countercultural, contrary to the ways of the world of big egos, pride, intolerance, and impatience.

Loving God and others is easier when things in our life are going well, but when we are facing difficulties, we tend to focus on ourselves and our circumstances rather than on God and others. When life's troubles and tribulations come knocking at our door, let us remember the most perfect way, the way of love.

I cannot think of a better example of love in action than Mother Teresa of Calcutta, founder of the religious order of the Missionaries of Charity and also a recipient of the Nobel Peace Prize. To her, living what Jesus said was simple. Jesus' words were all about love being put into action: "If you love me, you will obey what I command" (John 14:15) and love God with all your heart, all your soul, all your mind, and your neighbor as yourself" (see Matthew 22:37–39).

Mother Teresa saw God in every human being, responding to each one with all the love and devotion, all the attention and respect that God Himself deserves. She focused her initial attention on the most neglected people in society: those abandoned and left behind by their families, bereft and disposed of all things. She also attended to the homeless and the hungry, and especially to those dying in the streets of Calcutta and Mumbai. There, she founded homes for the dying, where the primary focus was to care for people's spiritual and mental needs rather than on heroic efforts to prolong their lives.

Her ministry expanded to include TB clinics, pregnancy care clinics, mobile leprosy clinics, shelters for the homeless and orphans, and soup kitchens. She also ventured into primary and secondary education, as well as into emergency and disaster relief. In 1965, the Missionaries of Charity branched out to other countries, opening homes in Venezuela, Tanzania, and even in developed and affluent countries including Italy, the United Kingdom, Australia, and the United States.

Everywhere this organization's missionaries went, they established their home in slum areas. Their vow of poverty required them to have few personal belongings (what would fit into a shoe box), to dress like the poor, and to live among them, eating what they had. They acquired a personal understanding of what it is to be poor. Being poor themselves also gave them greater credibility and positioned them better for their ministry.

In highly developed countries, poverty takes a different nuance, being not so much a poverty of lack of food, water, and shelter but poverty of spirit, of loneliness and abandonment, of discouragement and lack of meaning in life. In Mother Teresa's book, *No Greater Love,* she says, "poverty does not only consist of being hungry for bread, but rather it is a tremendous hunger for human dignity. The world today is hungry not only for bread, but hungry for love, hungry to be wanted and to be loved. The world hungers to feel the presence of Christ" ([*New World Library,* 2002], 93).

True love is a love of action and service. The deepest form of love is to love until we have no more to give. It is sacrificial and causes pain.

As Mother Teresa explains this truth in her book, "at the moment of death we will not be judged by the amount of work we have done but by the weight of love we put into our work. This love should flow from self-sacrifice, and it must be felt to the point of hurting" (140).

Love is what defines us as Christians. It is our emblem, our stamp and seal, our trademark. May we choose love to be our defining characteristic, what is most prominent and most notable about us. May our cup be filled with love to the brim, so that when life's problems bump us, our cup overflows and spills over love instead of hate. May we always choose love over hate.

CHAPTER 3

CHOOSE TO SERVE OVER BEING SERVED

To have a servant's heart for God is to allow God to use ordinary people, such as you and me, to do extraordinary things. We cannot within ourselves ever have enough qualifications, abilities, and aptitudes to do God's work. We have to present our meager human abilities to Him and be willing to be used by God to do great things.

I am reminded of the parable recorded in John 6 where Jesus feeds the multitude. The people were hungry and had nothing to eat, and a little boy had just a few fish and pieces of bread. Obviously what the boy had to offer was not enough to feed the multitude, but all God needed were those meager resources and the boy's willingness to give them. Similarly, God is able to multiply our limited skills and talents and use them for His purpose. All we have to do is to have a servant's heart for God and be willing to be used by Him. God then takes care of the details.

His Will Becomes Our Will

I have already said in chapter 1 that in order to have a heart for God, we must first be living in His will. I must say it again because it is fundamental and very basic. We have to first know God, which requires having a personal relationship with Him, learning His Word, and delighting in it. Without this foundation, we cannot do anything or be of service for His kingdom. We are useless to Him. When we have this foundation and are living in God's will, He is reflected in our lifestyles, our choices, our dress, and our speech.

Prayer, our means of communicating directly with God, is essential to living in His will. Our prayer life transforms us. By prayer, His will is imprinted upon our hearts. "He anointed us, set his seal of ownership on us, and put his Spirit in our hearts as a deposit" (2 Corinthians 1:22). When His will becomes our will, then we are able to be of use to Him.

Jesus, Our Example

According to the wisdom of the world, greater is he who is being served than the one who serves. God's wisdom is the opposite. Greater is the one who serves. As stated in Philippians 2:6–8, Jesus, "who, being in very nature God … made himself nothing, taking the very nature of a servant … humbled himself." Scripture also teaches that God gives grace to the humble and opposes the proud (see 1 Peter 5:5). Our role is to be imitators of Jesus. If He can take on the nature of a servant, so can we.

In order to be disciples of Christ Jesus, we must follow His example. As recorded in John 13, the Lord washed His disciples' feet as an example of humility. Serving others with humility, therefore, is to be ingrained in our DNA just as it was for Jesus.

To Bear Fruit

It is through service that we bear fruit. Scripture says in Matthew 7:17, "Every good tree bears good fruit." To bear fruit means to live a righteous life by being in a right relationship with God and with others. To live in right relationship with God and others is to love and serve them.

Loving others means looking after them, being mindful of their suffering and their needs. To ignore the suffering of others is unrighteous and the mark of a fruitless life. "Every tree that does not bear good fruit is cut down and thrown into the fire" (Matthew 7:19). To bear fruit, then, is to have works that give glory to God and that advance the kingdom of heaven. These works are not only soul winning but also service and being an example to others in that service.

Our Lord commanded his disciples to serve others, telling them, "be dressed ready for service and keep your lamps burning" (Luke 12:35). We must, therefore, seek opportunities for service and be vigilant not to miss them. No matter what our calling in life is, opportunities for service are numerous but not always recognized. Opportunities are presented to us daily in the form of needs that require giving of ourselves, our time, our talents, or our money. We must recognize the needs of others as opportunities presented to us by God, and we must be ready and willing to pour ourselves out as fragrant offerings into the service of others.

Outside of the Comfort Zone

It is easy for us to be deceived into believing that we are already serving the Lord in the routines of our daily lives and fail to step out of our comfort zone and do something great for God. Perhaps it is fear of failure, fear of the unknown, or fear of real or imagined risks that we fail to respond to the call for service. I can testify that in my own life as a new believer I failed many times to respond to the call for service through missions. Being a physician in practice in a medically indigent community, I thought that I already took care of the poor at home and that I did not need to worry about the poor abroad. I thought that surely there were other people to do that job. But one day God spoke to my heart about this issue. He asked me to stop making excuses, to get out of my comfort zone, and to do something more in His name.

I then went on my first mission trip to the Amazon jungle of Peru to serve the Aguaruna Indian tribe. Their needs and their suffering left a permanent mark in my soul. I found out how wrong I had been in thinking that there were other people to take care of the poor. It became evident to me that nobody was going to do the job that was mine to do. I realized that we all have responsibility for the poor and an obligation to help alleviate their suffering. I knew then that as followers of Jesus Christ, we must take our responsibility to heart and get out of our comfort zone and go do the job that is ours to do.

Since then, there has not been a day in which I do not think about missions. My wife, Carol, and I have now been on six medical mission trips to Peru, Papua New Guinea, and Swaziland, and we have ongoing community support programs in those countries.

Papua New Guinea

After our first mission trip to Papua New Guinea in 2003, God placed a burden on our hearts for the people and our mission hospital there. Upon our return home, God opened our eyes to the significant medical waste that we have in our country. This waste includes medical equipment and medical supplies that are still usable and in working order but are no longer in use. We asked our local hospitals to donate to the Kudjip Nazarene Hospital in Papua New Guinea all discarded or replaced equipment and supplies. To our surprise, they agreed. To date, we have sent four 40-foot containers of materials to the mission hospital.

This container project has extended the blessings of missions to our own church, as many members have prayed for, helped financially, or participated in the physically demanding job of packing the containers. It has also extended the blessing to the rest of the Southwest Ohio District of the Church of the Nazarene.

In order to elicit funds for the project, my wife and I have frequently been guest speakers on missions at many churches in our district. The response has been tremendous. For instance, our third container was in part financed by donations from the children that attended Vacation

Bible School at the eighty-five churches of the S.W. Ohio District during the summer of 2008.

I once thought that the efforts of a single human being could not possibly change the world. I now know that goodness toward others has a ripple effect, and that those who are touched on every mission trip then go on to touch others. In this way, goodness and love grow exponentially and can truly change the world.

My testimony is given here not to boast about my mission work, for surely there are others whose work far surpasses my humble efforts. My intention is rather to show an example of how easily we deceive ourselves into believing that we are already of service while comfortably ignoring the suffering of the world.

Clearly we cannot be comfortable while the world suffers. How can we ignore the death of millions of human beings in Africa from the HIV/AIDS epidemic and think that it is an African problem or perhaps God's punishment for promiscuity? How can we witness starving children eating mud cookies to satiate their hunger or thirsty children drinking dirty water to quench their thirst and still think that these are problems for other people to solve while we enjoy life in the most prosperous country in the world and do nothing about their suffering?

In the Service of Others

To choose to serve God is to become engaged and involved in helping relieve the suffering of the world in whatever ways God places on our heart. We cannot all physically go to areas of great suffering in the world, but we can participate in the work of others in those areas through our support of organizations that are at the forefront of the war on poverty, such as World Vision, Save the Children, and Life Water Wells, to name just a few.

To choose to serve others is to choose to do God's work. Nothing is more satisfying or rewarding than to be of use to the Master: to be His instrument, His hands, and His feet. It stands to reason that a created thing or creature would seek the Creator and seek to be part of His creation. In the service of others, the creature surrenders to the Creator, and becomes a co-participant in His work. When the creature is molded by the Creator into a useful instrument, it finds the utmost happiness and fulfillment of its purpose.

C.S. Lewis, in his book *The Problem of Pain* (HarperCollins, 2001), states that most of the world's pain is produced by man. Man created the weapons of destruction and pain. God did not. To serve others helps reverse man's created pain and reduces humanity's burden of pain. Perhaps nothing on earth can get us closer to the abundant life that is promised to those that seek first the kingdom of God as a life devoted to the service of others.

CHAPTER 4
CHOOSE HOPE OVER DESPAIR

A fifty-year-old woman came to my medical office with the complaint of vague abdominal discomfort and bloating. Numerous tests were performed that failed to reveal any abnormality. Still she was persistent in her complaint. I believed her and arranged for her to undergo an operation where a scope is inserted into the abdomen to visualize the internal organs. This time, the results were clear. She had advanced stage ovarian cancer.

The next step was for her was to receive the standard treatment for this condition, which included extensive surgery and chemotherapy. My gut feeling was that she would not survive for more than a year. To my astonishment, she survived more than ten years. She was never cured of the disease, but she lived with it.

What was most amazing about this woman was not that she lived ten years with the disease. What amazed me was her attitude. She chose hope over despair. Until the end, she believed that she could be cured. When her ten-year battle with cancer ended and she succumbed to the disease, her husband said, "She never gave up hope. She was a fighter."

Another patient of mine received the same diagnosis not long after the first one, having a similar stage of disease. Her attitude about her disease was completely different: she felt hopeless. She strongly believed that her condition was terminal and that all efforts to cure it would be futile. She could not be dissuaded. She refused all treatments and died a few months later. She had no hope.

These examples underscore the power of hope. Hope conditions our outlook on life. Hope's effects are powerful, even in seemingly impossible situations.

Confidence in God's Ability

To hope is to have confident expectation of the fulfillment of something we desire. Hope comes from confidence and trust in something beyond our circumstances. For believers, it comes from confidence in God's promises, in the knowledge that God is good to His word. Placing our trust in God's promises focuses our minds and hearts on God's unlimited ability, not our limited abilities. "Find rest, O my soul, in God alone; my hope comes from him" (Psalm 62:5).

Hope allows us to rise above any situation we face in life and see things from God's perspective. We can then wait upon the Lord and His perfect timing, refusing despair. "Those who hope in the Lord will renew their strength. They will soar on wings like eagles" (Isaiah 40:31).

To have hope is to allow God to be in control. It is to stand before the heavenly throne and be still before God, knowing that He understands our needs. It is to be confident that we are secure in His hands and can trust His promises.

Despair's Downward Spiral

To despair is not to trust in God, to think we are beyond His reach, to think He does not care or does not exist. Simply put, despair is from the Devil.

This chapter was written during the worst world economic crisis since the Great Depression, a time of widespread unemployment, business failures, and a financial services crisis. The daily news spoke of people losing their jobs, their homes, their life savings, and their dreams. It was a time of stress and struggle, gloom and doom. People were losing not only their possessions but also their hope and their faith, going into the downward spiral of despair and hopelessness.

All around the world, church attendance was declining and charitable donations dwindling. The higher developed world was seeing increasing hardship, while the underdeveloped world was experiencing incredible and unspeakable suffering. In many parts of the world, the panorama was of homelessness, of millions of unnecessary and preventable deaths from infectious diseases, from wars, and from government and state failures. To many it seemed to be the end of times.

Whenever the world faces a severe political, economic, or security crisis, its people stand at the crossroads between hope and despair. Often we must quickly make choices that will have long-lasting consequences. There is no time to lose. We cannot hesitate. We must be decisive.

Long is the road that leads to despair and hopelessness. Those who choose this road exhibit pessimism and negative thinking. Their choices are controlled by the specter of doom. They are prey to depression, addiction, and progressive mental, spiritual, and physical deterioration. Despair is the long, dark night of the soul.

The Road of Hope

Shorter, but not always easier, is the road of hope. Its way is encouraging and uplifting. It leads to confidence and dependence on the Lord—a dependence not on our own wisdom and efforts but on God's. As Solomon stated in Proverbs 3:5–6, "trust in the Lord with all your heart and lean not on your own understanding; in all your ways acknowledge him, and he will make your paths straight." Hope causes us to radiate positive thinking and exude optimism. Our outlook is good, the future seems bright, and our choices are driven by the light we picture just ahead. The night is nearly over, the morning near.

Hope is a choice we must make, a road we must travel in order to have abundant life. But it is also a gift we receive, not from our own merits but from trust in and dependence upon the Lord.

Loss of hope occurs when we lean only on our own power and trust only in the basic principles of this world. It happens when we look into the storm and not at Jesus. By our choice, we allow despair to plant its seed in our soul.

To those who have lost hope, I offer a recovery program. It is based on choosing to place complete and undivided trust in Jesus Christ. He is able, capable, and willing to care for us. By faith we trust in Him, and in return He gives us hope.

A Place of Hope

The village of Kudjip is located five thousand feet above sea level, perched upon a mountain in the Western Highlands Province of Papua New Guinea. Like many other places in this country, due to the rugged topography, Kudjip is not accessible by land from the capital city of Port Moresby. Travel to and from it depends on air access.

Papua New Guinea's social structure is tribal—polygamy is prevalent, tribal warfare common, and domestic violence frequent. School enrollment is low, with only 10 percent of girls attending grade school. Like in many other places of the third world, pregnancy can be a death sentence for women. As a result of the reproductive process, many die of unrecognized pregnancy related complications.

The Kudjip Nazarene Hospital is a symbol of hope for many people in Papua New Guinea. It provides health services for 250,000 people of the Highlands. There they find healing for their ailing bodies and also hope for their lives.

The hospital, along with its Community Health Network, is a beacon of light in an otherwise bleak and grim health panorama. It is the indispensable first and last resort for many of the citizens of the Highlands.

My wife and I have volunteered at the hospital on three different occasions. We have vivid memories of our service there: leading mission teams, showing the *JESUS* film to stunned villagers, working in construction projects, participating in Sunday services in bush churches, and doing our medical work at the hospital. We have many pleasant memories of the missionaries and their families, of the workers at the hospital, and of the patients.

We will not easily forget the night that a woman in shock was brought into the emergency department by her family. Pregnant with her first child, she had been in labor for three days and had been unable to deliver. Being unwed and feeling ashamed, she had been reluctant to seek care until late into the birthing process, even though she had been bleeding for three days. When she arrived at the hospital, her baby was dead, and she was barely clinging to life. She was rushed into the operating room for an emergency cesarean section. A stillborn infant was delivered. Despite blood transfusions, the woman's blood pressure remained dangerously low.

In the recovery room, nurses and doctors administered a Dopamine drip in order to raise her blood pressure and open up her kidneys, which had shut down. Little by little, color and life returned to her cheeks, and her blood pressure improved. She would live.

This woman's life was saved at the Nazarene Hospital and also her soul. During her stay, pastors ministered to her spiritual needs. She accepted Jesus Christ into her heart before she was discharged to go home.

The Kudjip Nazarene Hospital in Papua New Guinea is a place of healing, hope, and peace for the people of the Highlands. It dispenses hope for the earthly lives and also the hope that is eternal.

There has never been a better time to be invested in the gospel of hope and to have a hope that is eternal. Hope is not only about our life and what we will eat, but also about eternal life and sharing in God's glory. This is our everlasting hope. In the end, this hope is what matters most.

The choice before us is between hope and despair. One leads to light, the other to darkness. God's everlasting hope leads to eternal life. Without hope, despair leads to our own destruction. It is a very basic but all-important decision.

CHAPTER FIVE
CHOOSE JOY OVER SADNESS

She was a beautiful young Christian woman who had a serious condition. She had been admitted into the hospital the week before with a bowel condition that made her very sick, had undergone surgery, and seemed to be improving. At the time I was a young resident physician, and she was one of my patients.

All seemed well when I checked in on her that morning, but that night she took a turn for the worse and had horrible, life-threatening complications. She developed a bowel perforation and an overwhelming infection. I spent all night trying to improve her chances of recovery.

I had not slept when I presented her in morning rounds to the attending physicians. I looked and felt terrible. As I described the extent of her complications, my fellow physicians did not believe me. Her face was radiant and looked as if she had just redone her makeup. Nobody could look that good while being so sick, they thought. She died that morning.

At the time I wondered what she had in her life that could have made her so radiant. I was not a true believer, being only a nominal Christian; that is, I was one who called himself a Christian but was without a lifestyle that reflected it. It would be fifteen more years before I accepted Jesus into my heart and pledged to live the rest of my life for Him.

I never forgot the radiance of her face. I know now that it reflected God's presence: she had the joy of the Lord. She knew that no matter what her circumstances were and even in the face of death, she had something eternal that no one or nothing could take away.

Radiant Joy

I have a passion for missions. I love going overseas on short-term missions trips and working in the mission field as a medical missionary. One thing that has become very evident to me is the work of the Holy Spirit in new Christians, how the Spirit transforms their lives. They have a joy that is radiant and infectious. I can identify them even in a crowd, because the Spirit lights up their faces, and joy is evident in their demeanor. I can also tell those who have sin in their lives. It also shows in their faces.

I have come to believe that for many Christians, their religion has become a habit or a routine. They have become complacent; they lack fervor or enthusiasm; their faith has become stale. They appear gaunt and depressed, overwhelmed by the world. What is lacking is the work of the Spirit so that they too can radiate the joy that is evident in new Christians. They need a revival of the Holy Spirit.

Early Christian writings by church father Augustine (AD 354–430) define joy as a "song of the soul." According to Augustine, joy comes when we transcend our human nature and find ourselves in the presence of God.

The joy of the Lord is our strength! It is one of our most salient characteristics as Christians. This truth has been evident throughout the ages. It was evident from the beginning of Christianity during the Roman persecutions as those early Christians sang to the Lord while facing the lions, and it is still evident today.

Joy: the Presence of God

Contemporary Polish-Canadian writer Irma Zaleski defines joy as "the inner experience of the presence of God" (*The Inner Journey*, Parabola Anthology Series, Lorraine Kisly and others, eds. [Morning Light Press, 2006], 163). She states that all human beings must find their own way to joy. For most people, joy comes as glimpses of the eternal presence as we go through our lives. Zaleski also says that the presence of God can be found in all truth, beauty, and love. God is love, and love is the source of joy (167).

We became aware of the presence of God through prayer, which is conversation with God. Even when we pray without words and are silent before God, we also become aware of His presence. Silencing the mind may require practice and time, but even milliseconds of silence can have great value in understanding the transcendental reality of God. He becomes real and vivid, in all His power and all His glory. The burden is upon us to carry His presence into the reality of our daily living.

It is counterintuitive to try to explain silence, because silence requires no words; the more we attempt to explain it, the more it drifts away. Suffice to say that silence before God is a spiritual discipline worth practicing because it opens the door into His presence, where we find joy.

Receiving the Holy Spirit

Many people wonder where this infectious joy comes from, like I did as a young resident when I was struck by the expression of joy in my patient's face. They wonder what is it that others have that they can see. Some may even wonder if those who have it are mentally ill or under the influence of mind-altering drugs. No such thing! What they have is the Spirit of God at work in them. In the book of Acts (see 2:2), it is recorded that when the apostles were in the upper room, the Spirit of God descended upon them as a violent wind and tongues of fire. After that night, they were transformed people. It was reported that witnesses thought they were drunk. What a visible witness of the Holy Spirit in their lives!

Likewise, the most authentic witnessing we can offer to others is to allow the Spirit to transform us. We too can have radiant joy that is evident to all, that has nothing to do with our circumstances, that surpasses all understanding, and that even seems to be out of touch with reality.

What is more amazing is that this joy is part of the package we receive when we receive to Holy Spirit. The book of Galatians (5:22–23) states that "the fruit of the Spirit is love, joy, peace, patience, kindness, goodness, faithfulness, gentleness and self-control." Indeed it is quite an impressive package that we can receive by sincerely repenting of our sins, being forgiven, and accepting God into our lives. To be forgiven means that our debt from our sin is paid. It means we are free to leave our baggage of guilt and imperfection behind, and that sin no longer has a hold on us. As part of our forgiveness, we can then receive the Holy Spirit.

Happiness Is Not Joy

Joy is not the same as happiness. Joy comes from knowing God and asking and receiving forgiveness. Joy comes from the knowledge of our acceptance as children of God and our becoming heirs in His kingdom. Truly, the love of the King makes our hearts sing.

Happiness, in contrast to joy, comes from our circumstances, from the world. It comes from our ability to have a car and a job and to be able to pay our bills. Happiness is also from having a dog with a waggy tail and a house with a picket fence.

Sadness

Sadness comes from not having these things that bring happiness. It also comes from not having joy.

Sadness is a natural human emotion that may arise spontaneously, but more often it arises in response to negative experiences. Such experiences include personal loss, relationship loss or strain, financial crisis, humanitarian crisis or event, loss of a job, or loss of health or status.

Sadness that is incapacitating or extreme, that limits our ability to carry on the activities of daily living, is considered to be clinical depression. It is a medical condition that requires therapy. Many times this degree of sadness presents itself without precipitating cause or event and seems to have no explanation. Medical professionals know that it is has to do with the metabolism of substances in the brain called neurotransmitters.

Even Jesus felt sadness. The story of Lazarus tells us that our Lord was "deeply moved" and wept over his loss (see John 11:17–44).

Even though we will encounter sadness throughout the course of our lives, it should not be the most dominant or prevailing emotion. Sadness has its time and place. King Solomon, the writer of Ecclesiastes, states, "There is a time for everything, and a season for every activity under heaven ... a time to weep and a time to laugh" (3:1–4).

My Best Friend's Testimony

She lost her mother at six months of age and became orphaned at the age of six when her father suddenly died. From there on she was given to the foster care system. She grew up in two different foster homes until the age of eighteen, when she moved out and put herself through college.

The foster care system was a poor substitute for parents; in it she was not only unloved but also exploited and abused. Her faith was the only thing that sustained her during that difficult time. God's love was the only love she knew, and it was the only one she needed. It gave her great joy to be loved by the King, and to be called His child.

No friends or family attended her high school or college graduation ceremonies. Despite this lack of earthly support, she had peace in her heart because she knew God was there and He was all-sufficient; His presence gave her immense joy.

After we were married, it took years for her to recognize and trust my true love for her. At first it was a mixture of disbelief and uncertainty, but as time passed, she came to believe that it was possible to be loved by another person.

To her, joy is to be loved by God and to feel His presence. It is to know that His love is unconditional and irrevocable: no qualifications are needed to deserve it, and no one or nothing can take it away. This truth is what she hung onto again and again.

Being an orphan gave her unusual insight into what it is to be one. Her experience positioned her to be a very effective advocate for orphans. As a guest speaker at different churches, her powerful testimony was instrumental in securing the sponsorship, through World Vision, of over one hundred orphans of the HIV/AIDS epidemic in Africa. Together with our daughter and me, we now sponsor five orphans in Swaziland and two in Kenya.

In her life, she had a choice to make. She could easily have chosen sadness over what undoubtedly must have seemed the greatest tragedy anyone could endure in life, which was the loss of both parents at an early age. Instead, she chose joy: a joy that sustained her and gave her strength.

Her choice brings clarity to ours. Do we accept the Spirit of God into our hearts, the One who makes our joy complete and is radiant and infectious and evident to all? Or do we choose sadness, allowing worldly concerns and circumstances to be the ruler of our lives?

CHAPTER 6

CHOOSE HOLINESS OVER WORLDLINESS

He had an impressive resume. He attended the best schools and graduated at the top of his class. He lived in the best neighborhood and belonged to the country club. His spouse was a high profile professional. His was a high-income family. Many who envied his lifestyle said he had the "keys to the kingdom." Did he?

One does not obtain the keys to the kingdom by obtaining status in society or acquiring status symbols. Titles, possessions, and riches do not get us any closer to the true kingdom, the kingdom of God. In fact, they can be a hindrance. Scripture tells us that where our treasure is, so will our hearts be. If our hearts are focused and centered on attaining worldly recognition, we will be distracted from our main goal in life, which is to know God and to serve Him with all our hearts.

Attaining recognition or wealth is not evil in and of itself, but it should not be at the top our list, nor should it dominate our agenda or rule our lives. Holiness, not worldliness, should be our highest goal.

What Is Holiness?

Holiness begins by being consecrated and set apart for God. The Old Testament law teaches us that whatever is "given to the Lord becomes holy" (Leviticus 27:9). When we give ourselves to God, He consecrates us for His purposes. Only then can we begin to live a life of holiness.

Holiness is about doing God's will in our lives and not our own. Holy living, therefore, is the result of obedience to God.

God wants and expects a lot from us. He expects us to be instruments of love and instruments of change in the world. Changing the world toward righteousness requires making right choices. We cannot make those right choices unless we first are transformed by the gospel. The admonition in Romans 12:2 is clear: "Do not conform any longer to the pattern of this world, but be transformed by the renewing of your mind."

The pattern of this world is characterized by inequity, injustice, unfairness, and sin. The chaos we see in it is the result of the worldly choices of all humanity. Transformed people are not merely contemplative, passive individuals who do nothing about the injustices of the world. They are dynamic, action-oriented people who work to change the pattern of this world.

At the center of Christian teaching is the doctrine of the spiritual rebirth of a person by the confession of sins and the acceptance of Jesus Christ as Lord and Savior. Jesus said, "The Spirit gives birth to spirit ... 'You must be born again'" (John 3:6–7). In other words, being born again is required to enter the kingdom of heaven. A born-again person receives the Spirit of God, and the Spirit has transforming power. As it is stated in 2 Corinthians 5:17, "If anyone is in Christ, he is a new creation; the old has gone, the new has come!"

The gospel is clear in stating that faith and actions must work together. "Faith by itself, if it is not accompanied by action, is dead" (James 2:17). Therefore, our transformation will be evident by works that glorify God.

It is God who sets us apart and shows us the way of holiness just as He did at the beginning of the Christian era on the day of Pentecost. It is impossible for us to attain holiness by our own efforts, just as we cannot attain salvation by our own merits. It is a gift from God. Righteous choices and righteous living are affirmations that God lives in us.

As transformed people, we are called to change the world. We can change the world in the same ways twelve people did after being transformed by their meeting with Jesus of Nazareth twenty centuries ago.

The book of Acts contains the story of the disciples and the early church. It explains how Christianity grew from the testimony and efforts of a band of twelve fearful and scattered individuals into the largest religion in the world. After witnessing Jesus' death at the cross, His disciples witnessed His resurrection and His ascent into the heavens. At first they were afraid and uncertain about what to do, but their fear changed on the day of Pentecost. As they were gathered in the upper room of the house where they were staying, they "were filled with the Holy Spirit and began to speak in other tongues as the Spirit enabled them" (Acts 2:4).

From there on they were fearless, passionate, and unwavering in their desire to bring the good news of the gospel to the ends of the earth. Their story shows the transformation that takes place in individuals by the work of the Holy Spirit.

Worldliness Is Easily Recognizable

Worldliness is a term used to refer to the value systems of unbelievers and the moral values of the secular society in which we live. These values stand in distinct opposition to the values of believers. Jesus prayed to the Father about those who believed in Him, saying, "They are not of the world, even as I am not of it. Sanctify them by the truth; your word is truth" (John 17:16–17).

Worldliness is what causes pain and strife in our world. It translates into behavior that is easily recognizable: prideful, arrogant, boastful, easily angered, violent, deceitful, unfaithful, sexually immoral, perverse, and promiscuous. It is to be self-centered, self-seeking, and self-aggrandizing. "If then the light within you is darkness, how great is that darkness!" (Matthew 6:23).

The man mentioned at the beginning of this chapter appeared to be successful by the standards of this world and to have the keys to the kingdom, when in fact he did not. His life was filled with many riches, gains, recognition, and success; and he was also filled with worldly behaviors that revealed his true nature to those who knew him well.

The Way of Holiness

We live in constant spiritual warfare. The world is "enemy occupied territory," as C.S. Lewis states in his book, *Mere Christianity* ([HarperCollins, 2001], 46). We struggle against the power of evil. As the apostle Paul declared: "Our struggle is not against flesh and blood, but against the rulers, against the authorities, against the powers of this dark world and against the spiritual forces of evil in the heavenly realms" (Ephesians 6:12).

Through the ages, humanity has sought the path of holiness. Ascetics seek to obtain spiritual self-improvement by practicing self-denial, even of things that in themselves are good, such as warmth and comfort. Some cling to monastic life, that is, life confined to a monastery, in order to overcome the three great forces that the early Latin fathers of the church identified as the enemies of our soul: anger, lust, and laziness, also called the "noonday devil." This "noonday devil" is essentially those temptations that creep up in the mist of everything good we intend to do.

There are numerous examples of those who sought spiritual improvement through the monastic life: Saint Francis of Assisi and Saint Theresa of Avila, to name just two. Perhaps the path to holiness they chose was essential for them in their time. But we in our time can seek holiness in our daily lives without resorting to asceticism or monastic life. We need only embrace the truth that in Christ a new kind of person has appeared, a new creation: one "born again" through the Spirit, one that strives for holiness.

We may wonder, especially when sin creeps into our lives, if it is even possible to attain holiness in our lifetime. It is true that God created all human beings in His image—perfect, pure, and holy. Because of the original sin, which was the sin of disobedience, Adam and Eve were banished from the Garden of Eden (see Genesis 3:1–24). They failed to heed God's command and made the wrong choice. Sin had consequences, and because of their sin, every human being has inherited their sinful nature.

Nevertheless, God commanded His people in the Old Testament, long before Christ's coming, to "be holy, because I am holy" (Leviticus 11:44). Even though imperfection and sin were woven into humanity's basic makeup, God's plan for those He created did not change. The apostle Paul explained how we are set on the path of holiness once more. "The judgment followed one sin and brought condemnation" (Romans 5:16), but "just as through the disobedience of the one man the many were made sinners, so also through the obedience of the one man the many will be made righteous" (Romans 5:19).

Would God ask us to do something that He knew we were incapable of doing? Definitely not! What prevails: the sinful man or the new creation? It is our choice.

Clearly holiness is attainable, but it does not come instantly. For some it can be a long process, as old habits may die hard.

Some may say that holiness is too difficult. I disagree, because all of the work is done by God. As stated in 1 Thessalonians 5:23–24: "May God himself, the God of peace, sanctify you through and through. May your whole spirit, soul and body be kept blameless at the coming of our Lord Jesus Christ. The one who calls you is faithful and he will do it."

Holiness is not a once-and-for-all destination to reach. Just as health is maintained by making frequent healthy choices, holiness depends on making frequent, righteous choices and decisions. We are to offer ourselves regularly to "righteousness leading to holiness" (Romans 6:19). Holiness is a process, a work in progress, and a destination for our lives.

Jesus Is Our Example

Our most important decision on the path toward holiness is to follow Jesus. Jesus said, "I am the way and the truth and the life" (John

14:6). Our holiness journey starts when we first accept God into our hearts, at the moment we are born again. It then follows a path that leads us into discarding our old baggage and the habits that turn us away from God.

Jesus is the best model for our thinking and behavior. It is now popular among Christians in every situation to ask the question, "What would Jesus do?" It is a simplistic approach; nevertheless, it is a good place to start. John 13:15 states, "I have set you an example that you should do as I have done for you." Certainly we cannot go wrong by being imitators of God.

Wholesome behavior starts with wholesome thinking. It starts by placing God's Word in our hearts. I cannot stress enough the importance of spending daily time in devotion and studying God's Word, because God's Word is the road map for our journey in life.

C.S. Lewis states in *Mere Christianity* that "a Christian is not a man who never goes wrong, but a man who is enabled to repent and pick himself up and begin over again after each stumble" (63). In other words, on the road to holiness, there will be obstacles that cause us to stumble and fall. But as Christ enables us, we will be able to pick ourselves up and make a fresh start.

In addition to getting our thinking in order, our life choices and actions must reflect the truth, which is defined as being consistent with fact and reality. Our choices and actions also must be consistent with God's revelation. Holiness is dependent upon being surrounded and enveloped by the truth. Being set apart by God translates into obvious and recognizable behaviors: it is to be humble, patient, and kind; to rejoice with the truth; to be faithful, impartial, and sincere; and to bear good fruit. "By their fruit you will recognize them" (Matthew 7:16) essentially means that holiness is evident by the fruit we bear.

When everything has been said and done and the last page of our history has been turned, each of us will be judged by what we did with the truth given to us by God, which teaches us how to live in holiness. If the truth rules our lives and we are fervent and faithful to live in obedience to it throughout our lives, we will receive our reward from the Master. Matthew 25:19–21 teaches us this basic principle in the parable of the loaned money.

> After a long time the master of those servants returned and settled accounts with them. The man who had received the five talents brought the other five. "Master," he said, "you entrusted me with five talents. See, I have gained five more." His master replied, "Well done, good and faithful servant! You have been faithful with a few things; I will put you in charge of many things. Come and share your master's happiness!"

A Case in Point

Before we can change the world, God has to change us. Here is the story of one of my patients whom I have known for several years and whose progress has filled my heart with joy.

She was an attractive woman in her mid-thirties who always wore a business suit and lots of makeup and was very career and success oriented. Being an achiever, she had a Type A personality with little patience for mediocrity. She was harsh and aggressive and seemed to relish conflict. Her friends were carefully chosen, more often for their assets and portfolio than for the content of their character. She enjoyed the life of the rich and famous, with frequent trips to New York and Aspen.

The morning commute to work took her past a large evangelical church in her neighborhood, but her Christianity was superficial and did not include Sunday services. She believed in God but did not truly know Him.

Life seemed to smile upon her; she was on top of the world. But all that changed the day she lost her job. Soon her credit cards were maxed out, and she could no longer pay her bills. In despair, she sunk into a deep depression. The idols she had worshipped all of her life—money, fame, lifestyle, "things"—turned out to be false and could not rescue her. Neither did her friends, who also deserted her.

The person I saw at my office sitting across the desk was a shadow of her former self. Gone were the business suits and makeup, and she appeared disheveled, unkempt, and defeated. I treated her depression and also prayed with her. As we prayed that day, it became obvious to her that she had been looking for peace in all the wrong places. Her false idols had come tumbling down. She was ready for a new start.

Weeks later she told me that as she drove past the neighborhood church one Sunday morning, she could hear the choir and marveled at how its songs seemed very peaceful to her. She longed to feel that peace. That time she stopped. As she entered the church, she felt at first a bit strange and out of place. After a while she began to feel God's presence and peace. It was unlike anything she had felt in a very long time. She knelt at the altar and poured her heart out to God. She then accepted Jesus into her heart.

From then on, her priorities changed. She noticed the homeless in the streets, which had been previously invisible to her. She became the director of a homeless shelter. She had more joy in her life than ever before.

Her worldliness had left her empty, frustrated, and depressed. Her new life in Jesus transformed her from a selfish, ambitious, and aggressive person into one who overflows with joy and peace. She went from being a taker to being a giver, from being one who expected people to do things for her to one who did things for others. She went from worldliness to holiness, and now she bears fruit.

The Choice of Holiness

Life is a journey. As we walk on the road, we must be obedient to God's commands because obedience leads to righteousness (see Romans 6:16). Righteousness is the road that leads to holiness (see

Romans 6:19) and holiness to eternal life (see Romans 6:21). On this road will be obstacles that cause us to stumble and fall, but we must stay on the road, trusting God to give us what we need to continue on this lifelong journey.

Let us set our spiritual GPS correctly and mark well our destination. Let us choose holiness instead of worldliness. Our journey will then be not only spiritually rewarding and satisfying but also truly transformational.

CHAPTER 7
CHOOSE FAITH OVER DOUBT

Her phone rang in the middle of the night. The voice on the other end said, "You need to come to the hospital now. Your baby is dying." She was frantic as she hurriedly got herself ready and left the house. One hour later she was holding the lifeless body of her son, who had been born with a life-threatening birth defect. She sat there in silence, trying to analyze and process the situation. The God who created us and loves us had allowed this horrible tragedy to take place, she thought. At the same time, a voice within her said, "It's going to be okay. Have faith. Do not be afraid."

It is at times such as this one that our faith proves to be essential for survival. When our whole world is sinking around us, faith is the life raft we hang onto; it is our only way out of the deep water. If we do not have faith, we sink into the turmoil.

"Faith is being sure of what we hope for and certain of what we do not see" (Hebrews 11:1). It can also be defined as absolute trust or confident hope. Faith is what sustains us in times of trouble. Scripture tells us "the righteous will live by faith" (Galatians 3:11) because faith is the lifeline that connects us to the Father.

Justification through Faith

The Protestant Reformation that took place in Europe in the 1500s, led by Martin Luther, cleared the way for the acceptance of a biblical truth that had not received the attention it deserved. In his autobiography, Luther described a sudden flash of insight, a sort of revelation, when he read Romans 1:17: "For in the gospel a righteousness from God is revealed, a righteousness that is by faith from first to last, just as it is written:'The righteous will live by faith'."This truth became obvious to him: our justification, or salvation, is obtained through faith, by grace, a free gift from God, and not as a result of our works. This truth conflicted with the official Roman Catholic doctrine of justification by works, and it led to a division within the church that persists today (*Key Thinkers in Christianity* [Oxford University Press, 2003], 54).

Ephesians 2:8–9 says, "For it is by grace you have been saved, though faith—and this not from yourselves, it is a gift from God—not by works, so that no one can boast." Faith and its manifestation, works, are parts of the same instrument. Christian theologian C.S. Lewis compares their relationship to the two blades of a pair of scissors. One is useless without the other; they are effective only when they move together (*Mere Christianity* [HarperCollins, 2001], 148).

Faith is, therefore, not only our lifeline to the Father in times of trouble but also the instrument of our salvation. Without it, we cannot enter the kingdom of God.

The Healing Power of Faith

Faith is more than a lifeline and the instrument of our salvation. Faith is also a power tool. Through faith we are healed. Time and time again, the gospel tells us the source of healing. "Your faith has healed you" (Matthew 9:22). In other words, unless we have faith, we cannot be healed. God only asks that we believe.

As a medical doctor, I have faced many situations in which patients fail to improve despite the best science and technology. No matter what is done for them, they continue to deteriorate. There is no better time for prayer than in these situations, for prayer is faith expressed.

I will never forget that night not so long ago when I received an urgent call from the lab. The caller said, "All your patient's lab results are completely abnormal."

There was something very seriously wrong, I thought. She did not appear to be sick. In fact, she had spent the day decorating the room for her newborn, who was to arrive the next day by C-section. Unfortunately the test results were correct, and soon she took a turn for the worse. She had a seizure after her C-section caused by a brain hemorrhage. She then lapsed into a coma.

The outcome looked grim. Her situation could go either way, but full recovery seemed unlikely. Due to the location and size of the bleed, experts predicted possible paralysis and blindness. But the voice within, this time to me, said, "Have faith. Do not be afraid."

Word of her condition spread through family and friends. There was an outpouring of prayer in our town and in many cities around the world. Individuals who did not even know her and people in many churches were moved by her predicament and prayed fervently. On the third day of her coma, the woman woke up. She had weakness in one side of her body and could only see shadows. The prayers continued. Over the next three weeks, she experienced complete recovery and was able to walk out of the hospital.

I cannot say it more strongly or vehemently. Here was a person close to death or to serious neurological disability who experienced complete recovery, thanks to the power of faith and prayer.

Even a small amount of faith can go a long way. It can be as small as a mustard seed, says the Lord (see Matthew 17:20), and yet it is capable of moving mountains.

A Faith That Sustains

Doctor Bill McCoy is a career medical missionary at the Kudjip Nazarene Hospital in Papua New Guinea. As the hospital's medical director and as a family practice physician in the adult medical ward, he works long hours. Despite fatigue and tiredness, he is jovial, with an easy smile and a warm greeting for anyone he meets: "Apinoon" (good afternoon).

In his free time, he jogs around the hilly mission compound and tends to his half-acre vegetable garden. Vegetables and fruits grow colorful, large, and tasteful in the fertile volcanic soil of Papua New Guinea. He generously shares his crops with friends and other missionary families.

One day his day to be on call starts off very busy. He has to skip his morning jog and devotions to respond to an urgent call summoning him to the hospital's emergency department. A boy in his early teens has been brought in because he is complaining of lower extremity weakness and difficulty walking. He has to be carried in by his parents.

After the doctor completes a quick assessment, the young boy is diagnosed as having Gillain-Barre' syndrome—a life-threatening, progressive, neurological disorder that causes paralysis. He deteriorates rapidly. His paralysis soon extends to his respiratory muscles. When he turns blue and starts foaming at the mouth, Dr. Bill promptly places a tube down his windpipe. In many places of the third world, a complication such as this one is fatal. Because of the lack of equipment and of trained respiratory therapy personnel, mechanical support of respiration over an extended period of time is simply not possible. The outlook for this young boy seems grim.

The boy's lungs need to be ventilated using a manually compressed bag, much as a bellows, called an ambu bag. The compressions need to be given twenty times per minute, twenty-four hours a day. The breathing tube also must be cleared of mucous and secretion every hour by means of a suction device. This physically demanding and stressful job is assigned to students from the Nazarene College of Nursing. They take two-hour shifts.

It is necessary to transport the patient to the capital city of Port Moresby, as it is the only city in the country that has ventilators. Due to the rugged topography of the country, there are no roads connecting Kudjip to the capital city. The patient must be taken there via air transport. Regrettably there are no air ambulances available in Papua New Guinea.

Mission Aviation Fellowship is called upon to help. It is a dangerous and risky proposition. Their two-seater Cessna aircraft is hardly suited for this emergency. After careful thought and prayer, it is determined to be the only hope for the patient. With prayer, faith, and hope, the young boy is strapped into the front seat with his breathing tube securely taped in place. An attendant crawls into the cramped space behind the seat in order to continue providing the twenty compressions per minute to the ambu bag. A portable suction device is carried along for the trip, but no thought is given to how to clear the tube in flight, or how to reinsert the tube should it become dislodged.

The one and a half hour trip is uneventful. The boy is then transported to the general hospital, where he is placed on a ventilator. After three weeks of respiratory support, the patient's muscles recover enough that the tube can be removed. He makes a full recovery.

This young man stated that his faith was the only thing that sustained him during those long, difficult weeks. Many consecutive miracles were necessary for his survival. God's hand was in each one of them. The faith of his physician and his own personal faith were the necessary ingredients for his miraculous survival.

Healing Comes from God

It is important for all of us to recognize the connection between faith and healing, and to realize that healing only comes from God. We must recognize that doctors and nurses and other healthcare professionals are only instruments in the hands of the Great Physician.

I think often of the sign that stands in front of the Kudjip Nazarene Hospital in Papua New Guinea. It reads: "We treat. Jesus heals." Simple words, it seems, but words that contain great wisdom because they point toward the source of all healing—God.

The Price of Doubt

Doubt, on the other hand, hinders us and limits us from attaining God's full grace. When we doubt, we question God's love, God's power, and His ability to do what He has promised. In essence, doubt is synonymous with disbelief. When we doubt, we are essentially saying that God is not able, capable, or willing to help us or to rescue us. "But the man who has doubts is condemned … and everything that does not come from faith is sin" (Romans 14:23).

"Stop doubting and believe" (John 20:27) is Jesus' admonition to His disciple Thomas. The same message applies to all of us. We must have faith, believe, and not doubt. The price of not doing so is not one we want to incur.

The Source of Our Faith

How can we have a faith that saves, heals, sustains, and can move mountains? First we must hear the message of salvation contained in the gospel of Jesus Christ and believe. "Faith comes from hearing the message, and the message is heard through the word of Christ" (Romans 10:17). The message is like a seed that falls on fertile ground; it must then grow into faith, nourished and nurtured by the discipleship and fellowship of the church and fellow believers.

When faith has grown, it manifests itself by deeds that give glory to God. Faith is not a treasure to be locked up in a box where no one can see it, but it is to be displayed openly for the whole world to take notice. In other words, our good deeds are the most powerful and impacting testimony of our faith. "Let your light shine before men, that they may see your good deeds and praise your Father in heaven" (Matthew 5:16).

One of the most striking statements Jesus made about faith is recorded in Matthew 21:21: "I tell you the truth, if you have faith and do not doubt, not only can you do what was done to the fig tree, but also you can say to this mountain, 'Go, throw yourself into the sea,' and it will be done." In other words, we too have this amazing power within us, but only if we believe and have faith.

It is our choice. May we have a faith that saves and heals, a faith that sustains us and others, and that can move mountains. May the full record of our lives reflect our faith and be a living testimony for others to follow.

CHAPTER 8
CHOOSE GIVING OVER RECEIVING

Aurelius Augustinus was born in North Africa, in what was the Roman province of Numidia Proconsularis, in the year 354 of our era. Born to a well-to-do but not rich family, he received an exceptional education in Latin rhetoric. He became an avid reader, a prolific writer, and an eloquent speaker in a time and place where less than 10 percent of the population was literate. His life story can be seen as one of seeking and receiving and also as one of giving and sharing.

Monica, his mother, was a Christian believer, while Patricius, his father, was a pagan who later converted to Christianity. From his mother he received Christian instruction and upbringing; from his father he received his worldliness. Young Augustine was similar to other people of his age and time; he was rowdy, irreverent, and frivolous. Sometimes he would get in trouble with his friends, participating in wanton stealing for the sake of stealing, without any motive. After his conversion, this experience became the basis for his discussion on the nature of sin in his book *Confessions*.

Confessions is Augustine's autobiography and also an important theological text. In it he relates how his life completely changed after his conversion. (A conversion can be understood as the fundamental change that takes place in a person after receiving salvation, much like what happens after being "born again.") Like a person who is lost and then rescued and cannot stop thanking his rescuers, Augustine cannot stop thanking his Savior for salvation. For the rest of his life, he cannot stop thinking, writing, or speaking about God. Nor can he stop giving to others the knowledge of the truth that is found in

Jesus Christ. Giving to others the gift received is a fundamental biblical principle that is clearly displayed in Augustine's life.

His life can also be seen as a man's spiritual journey in search for the truth—looking for the "peaceful homeland" that can only be found in God. Augustine states that trying on his own, the path to the "peaceful homeland" is fraught with sin and failure; the path directed by God, however, leads to wisdom and truth. He says that "one can try in vain to make one's way over impassible ways surrounded by lurking and plotting" but "it is another thing to keep to the path that leads to the peaceful homeland, a path guarded under the care of the Heavenly Emperor" (*Confessions* VII, 27).

Augustine is, with good reason, an important theologian of the early Christian church. To him the greatest gift a person can receive is the knowledge of God and the salvation offered to man in the gospel of Jesus Christ. Telling others about it is also the greatest gift we can give.

Augustine's life illustrates two important points. One is that seeking our own path without God is fraught with failure; only with God can we reach the "peaceful homeland" and abundant life. The second is that having found the truth, we must give it to others.

One may ask, what can a person give that God did not give first? "Obviously, O God, all things come from You" (Augustine, *Confessions* I, 7). This is an apt question to frame this chapter on giving. It points to God as the source of all things we both give and receive.

Receiving Is Easy

Most of us like receiving. We are enthusiastic receivers and are always ready to receive love, money, gifts, recognition, and praise. Nevertheless, abundant life does not come from receiving but from giving. Here is an apparent paradox: When we give certain gifts, we have more instead of less because what we give is replenished; we always have more to give. Sounds strange, no doubt, but it is completely true.

It begs the question, what is it that we can give that replenishes itself and we always have more of it to give? Love is such a gift. The more love we give, the more we receive. Expressions of love include gifts of our money, time, and skills.

Giving Can Be Just as Easy

Few of us are enthusiastic givers. Let's face it. Some people are stingy, especially with their money. They erroneously think that the more they save it and keep it, the more they will have. Perhaps this idea is true in the wisdom of the world and its way, but it is not true from an eternal perspective.

God rewards a faithful giver. There is no question that the gates of heaven open up and we receive one blessing after another when we give generously. In Malachi 3:10 we read: "'Test me in this,' says the Lord Almighty, 'and see if I will not throw open the floodgates of heaven and pour out so much blessing that you will not have room enough for it.'" If anyone has doubt, let him put this principle to the test.

God Is Able to Meet Our Needs

God is the Creator and giver of life. As Augustine said, all good things come from Him. "He who supplies seed to the sower and bread for food will also supply and increase you store of seed and will enlarge the harvest of your righteousness" (2 Corinthians 9:10). God provides for our needs: our health, our work and rest, our home and shelter, our skills and our success, and also our money. We should not hesitate to give generously in return, because God is able to meet all our needs.

Not only does God provide for our needs, but He also gives us resources to invest for Him. We are His hands and feet to make the most of what He provides. He expects us to be wise stewards of what

He has given us and to use our resources not only for our benefit but for the benefit of others. "Whoever sows sparingly will also reap sparingly, and whoever sows generously will also reap generously" (2 Corinthians 9:6). As we "sow," we must always keep in mind where our resources come from and the One gave them to us first. We must then be generous in giving our resources to others.

God does not need our money. What He needs is our obedience and willingness to give of ourselves to others with a gentle heart, being mindful of their needs. What we give is not as important as how we give it—the attitude of our heart.

Giving of Our Time

More precious than money, for a lot of us, is our time. Giving of our time is giving of ourselves, actually giving a portion of our lives away. It shows how much we care. It is the most authentic type of witnessing we can do. It speaks volumes about our faith, and it is more eloquent than words. The gospel states that we should not be content with saying "I wish you well; keep warm and well fed" while doing nothing to help those in need (James 2:16). We cannot be effective witnesses by just our words. Giving of our time is essential.

Giving of our time is not only essential, but it is irreplaceable. It cannot be substituted for by anything else. Giving of our time may mean something as simple as listening to another person's story, being an empathetic listener; or it may mean something as complex as traveling overseas to serve in the mission fields of the third world.

Actions Speak Louder than Words

We can give of our time, allowing our actions to speak louder than our words through volunteering. Stuffing envelopes for a charity organization's mailing and stacking donated food on the shelves of a food pantry are a few examples. Other volunteer opportunities, however, allow us to donate both our time and our skills, giving them freely and without a charge, and expecting nothing in return. We can volunteer where our skills best match a need, or we can volunteer where the need is greatest. It can be in our neighborhood or in our town, in soup kitchens or shelters. It can be in our own country or half way across the world.

I personally prefer to volunteer abroad, for that is where the need is greatest. My skills as a physician and my wife's as a nurse are literally life changing there for people who have little or no access to health care. I cannot remember any more spiritually rewarding or satisfying time than the time my wife and I spent in the mission fields of the third world.

Poverty is different in different parts of the world. In our country we have a social safety net that protects our poor. It includes food pantries, soup kitchens, clothing banks, homeless shelters, shelters for abused women, Section 8 housing assistance, food stamps, unemployment compensation, Medicaid, and Social Security Disability Insurance.

In stark contrast, there is no social safety net in the third world; there, poverty is even more dramatic and impacting. Consider, for instance, poverty so abject and so profound that a person has nothing to wear, nothing to eat, nowhere to sleep, and no place to go when sick. This degree of extreme poverty is rarely seen in our country; sadly, it is common and prevalent in the third world.

Here in this country, wherever we volunteer, our actions speak quietly to those in need that they are not alone in their suffering, that God cares for them and provides for them in their need. When we volunteer in the third world, our actions scream out this message.

Sacrificial Giving

Even harder, but more beautiful, is to give sacrificially. Sacrificial giving is giving not out of our abundance, but out of our want. It is giving to others to the extent that we are in need. This giving honors God even more.

The greatest example of sacrificial giving is recorded in Matthew 27:50, as our Lord Jesus with a loud voice gave up His Spirit as atonement for our sins. Without a doubt, that was the greatest gift of all time, one that we freely received. It is also one that we can share with others.

Years ago after a mission trip to the Amazon Jungle of Peru, I came home with a burden to help a young boy I had met there. He'd had his leg amputated after stepping in an animal trap in the jungle. In the jungle of Peru, there are many amputees without prostheses, the result of snakebites or accidents. This boy was discouraged because he had outgrown his prosthesis and could not walk to school. To buy him a new prosthesis in Peru would cost $1,500.

One Sunday I spoke at my church in Ohio about this need. After the service, a Christian brother of mine gave me a check for the full amount. I will never forget that gift because my friend was not wealthy and could not afford to give this gift. It was obviously sacrificial. He had a large family and at the time was driving a beat-up car and needed a new one. That Sunday, thanks in part to my friend's sacrificial giving, twice the amount needed was donated. All of it was remitted to Peru.

A few months later, I received news and pictures of the young boy with his new prosthesis. The funds were not only enough for him, but they had also helped two other amputees to receive prostheses.

We Receive More than We Give

My friend who gave sacrificially continued to drive his beat-up car, but God amply rewarded him in his family and personal life. Years later in his mid-fifties, he was able to retire from working as a schoolteacher. He now devotes his time to vocational activities and volunteering.

The story doesn't end there. The young boy who received the new prosthesis later became a pastor of the church of the Nazarene. He now serves the Lord in the Amazon Jungle of Peru.

This example illustrates how giving benefits not only the receiver but also the giver. It shows how the blessing of giving is extended to benefit others beyond anything we could have ever imagined.

Let us return to the question at the beginning of this chapter, what can a person give that God did not give first? Think about it and make the right choice, knowing that it is more blessed to give than to receive.

CHAPTER 9

CHOOSE STRENGTH OVER WEAKNESS

Like a muscle that is not used atrophies, so does the spirit that is not nourished. It becomes progressively weaker. Weakness causes fatigue, and fatigue renders it incapable of completing the tasks before it.

Highly competitive runners devote time preparing for the race ahead. Every day they carefully and systematically train to build up their strength and increase their endurance. They work to improve their performance, seeking to achieve their goals in progressively less time. Like athletes in training, we must choose to pursue what gives us strength in order to live the abundant life.

An Exceptional Athlete

My closest encounter with a highly competitive athlete occurred during my high school years. From 1963–1966, I was enrolled at the Northfield Mount Hermon School in Mount Hermon, Massachusetts. The school, a nondenominational Christian high school, was founded by Dwight L. Moody, a famous evangelist of the nineteenth century. There I received some of the most important and enduring spiritual teachings of my life. At the time I liked to run, and I was on the cross-country team as well as the track and field team.

In my cross-country group was a young man who was an above average runner. He persistently ran in front of the pack and always, at the last lap, he would make a mad dash to the finish line, winning the race every single time. His running technique was impeccable, one that I tried to emulate with little success. He knew how to pace himself, sometimes slowing down to conserve energy, sometimes picking up the pace in an unbelievable crescendo, just when everyone else had no more energy to give. He had, in addition, an incredibly long stride. He was the assured victor at every competition.

Upon his graduation from high school, this young athlete went on to Yale University. I lost track of his career and accomplishments until the 1972 Summer Olympic Games in Munich, Germany. There he received the gold medal in the men's marathon. It was quite an accomplishment for any athlete, but more significantly for one who had his humble beginnings in a small New England boarding school. His name: Frank Shorter.

I am privileged to have run with Frank Shorter, an exceptional athlete. I am even more privileged, however, to run my race of life with Jesus Christ, the source of my strength. Here is an important choice everyone must make in life: to choose to run the race with Jesus, who gives us strength.

To Run and Not Be Weary

We who follow Jesus need to prepare for the race set before us (see Hebrews 12:1). We must increase our strength, building up our spiritual endurance. We need to train so that we can perform our tasks with success. Our goal is to finish the race and achieve the crown of glory. "Run in such a way as to get the prize ... do it to get a crown that will last forever" (1 Corinthians 9:24–25).

We increase our spiritual strength by spending time in the presence of the Father, who gives rest to our spirits and restores our souls (see Psalm 23:2–3). Through Him we receive spiritual "manna" that nourishes us as we pass through the deserts of life (see John 6:32–33). "Those who hope in the Lord will renew their strength. They will soar on wings like eagles" (Isaiah 40:31a). With Him we can soar through life's troubles and tribulations. We can "run and not grow weary ... walk and not be faint" (40:31b).

We also increase our spiritual strength by knowing God's Word and obeying what it says. "Let the word of Christ dwell in you richly as you teach and admonish one another with all wisdom" (Colossians 3:16). God gives us the right and responsibility to make choices about how we spend our lives. Of the many choices we can make in life, obedience to what we read in His Word is the most fundamental to fully enjoy abundant life. The choice to obey Him determines whether we live in the full light of God's love and receive His blessings or vanish into darkness.

In Deuteronomy 28, the Israelites are presented with the choice to obey God or to choose their own way. They are told what the outcome will be if they choose to obey. "If you fully obey the Lord your God and carefully follow all his commands ... All these blessings will come upon you and accompany you" (verses 1–2). The choice to obey Him would enable them to go into the Promised Land, but the choice to go their own way would make them weak and unable to enjoy the abundant life He had before them.

Our spiritual strength is further built up by church attendance, enjoying the fellowship of other Christians. "The body is a unit, though it is made up of many parts; and though all its parts are many, they form one body. So it is with Christ. For we were all baptized by one Spirit into one body" (1 Corinthians 12:12–13). The church nurtures us and spiritually disciples us. Church activities increase our spiritual stamina.

Finally, our spiritual strength is built up by occupying our minds with things eternal. "Set your minds on things above, not on earthly things" (Colossians 3:2). This part of our training to run the race set before us involves choosing what builds us up while rejecting what tears us down. By reading wholesome books and viewing clean entertainment, for example, we deny the enemy of our souls a footing where to stand. Likewise, we may choose to become knowledgeable in a foreign language or culture or to become an expert in a particular part of the world. We may choose to study and understand a particular human problem or condition that cries out to the heavens to be solved.

Finding Purpose for Our Life

Our spiritual strength finds its focus when we find our spiritual gifts and the purpose for which we were created. God created us for a reason and with a purpose. Nobody is created without such a purpose. "I have raised you up for this very purpose" (Exodus 9:16). To fulfill our purpose, we are created with a unique set of characteristics that makes us uniquely suited for the race ahead. It is our duty to find the purpose for our life and use our unique gifts to run the race before us.

Victor Frankl, author of the best-selling book *Man's Search for Meaning,* and a survivor of the Holocaust, states: "The true meaning of life is to be discovered in the world rather than within man" ([Beacon Press, 2006], 110). In other words, we find ourselves when we give ourselves to others.

According to Frankl, we can find meaning in life by the following:

1. "Creating a work or doing a deed" (111). That is, we can serve a cause greater than us, such as the Salvation Army, the Peace Corps, or World Vision.
2. "Experiencing something such as beauty, love, or truth" (111). The point here is that experiencing beauty (such as in Jesus) or experiencing love (whether human love or the love of God) or experiencing the truth (such as the truth that is in the gospel of Jesus Christ) gives tremendous meaning to life.
3. "The attitude we take toward unavoidable suffering" (111). Depending on what attitude we choose, we can turn into a victory of the human spirit what would otherwise be a tragedy that cannot be changed.

Spiritual Strength through Service

Just as athletes maintain their strength by regular exercise, we maintain our spiritual strength by serving others. In the service of others we define, develop, and refine the principles that motivate and guide our thoughts and our actions. These principles are entirely based on the gospel of Jesus Christ: of love for all human beings and love for God our Father; and of compassion and charity, giving comfort to those that suffer from the comfort we ourselves have received (see 2 Corinthians 1).

In the service of others, we experience firsthand in many tangible and intangible ways the power of the gospel to transform lives, and we develop deep-seated convictions about its power to transform society and change the world.

Jessica's Story

I first met Jessica, (name changed to protect her privacy) in my medical practice when she was referred to me for a hysterectomy. In her mid-thirties, she was subjected to irregular bleeding that was frequent, heavy, and sometimes constant. Tests showed that she had cervical cancer. As we prepared her for surgery, she shared her story.

Jessica had three children by different fathers. She had been addicted to cocaine and heroin. In order to satisfy the cravings of her drug addiction, she had resorted to stealing and prostitution. She had ended up in jail and lost custody of her children. After serving her time in prison, she was released broken, homeless, and alone. She had lost all the meaningful relationships in her life.

For months she lived in the streets with other homeless people with whom she shared drugs, sex, and alcohol. These "friends" would sometimes protect her and sometimes steal from her. She felt desperate. Her life had hit bottom. She was ready for a change.

One day while walking the streets, Jessica found herself in front of a faith-based homeless shelter appropriately named "Chosen." With tears running down her cheeks, she told me that it was there that she met Jesus. It was there she learned that God loved her and had given His life for her. It was there she learned that she was "chosen" of God, and what society had cast away as useless was precious to Him.

After several months in the shelter, she was found in a pool of blood. The director referred her to me for care. She underwent the much-needed surgery and returned to the shelter for recovery.

At this point, Jessica had a choice to make: to continue the downward spiral of her life or to begin a new life in Jesus. She understood that, whereas she had been weak before in her life, she now had strength in Jesus. She had His strength to overcome her addiction.

Jessica chose well. She now works at the shelter, bringing other homeless people to Christ and will never go back to the streets. Her life is changed forever.

Seeing God in Our Weakness

Sometimes the burdens of life are too heavy for us to carry. We are not strong enough and feel overwhelmed. We feel crushed and defeated, hopeless and lonely. In these times of great suffering and great sorrow, we need to cry out as Jesus did: "Abba, Father!" (Mark 14:36). We may not even know what to pray for, but "the Spirit himself intercedes for us with groans that words cannot express" (Romans 8:26). God's voice strengthens us in these times of weakness. His voice within us reminds us of His presence in every circumstance. "I am God, the God of your father ... Do not be afraid" (Genesis 46:3).

Sometimes we do not see God in the middle of a storm, but when we look back we can see that He was with us, that He carried us through it. I remind myself in times like these of the poem about the footprints in the sand. When we walk through a storm, we may see only one set of footprints, ours, and wonder where God is. As we look back later on, however, we recognize the truth. Those footprints are not ours but His as He carried us through the storm.

Rescue by Divine Intervention

One of the most dramatic rescue stories in the Bible is contained in the book of Daniel. Daniel, God's faithful servant, lived twenty-five centuries ago, but his story is relevant to us today. After the fall of the kingdom of Judah, Daniel, along with thousands of his countrymen, was sent into exile in Babylon. He was condemned to death in two separate occasions: once by fire and the second time by being placed in a den of hungry lions. Both times God rescued him.

Like Daniel, there are times when we need God's intervention to rescue us from great physical or spiritual harm. We are rescued, not because of our merits, but because of God's grace.

I remember one such occasion of God's divine intervention when I was a college student. I had been elected class representative to the student council. At the time, South America was engulfed in intense political turmoil. These were the days of Ernesto "Che" Guevara's guerrilla warfare in the jungles of Bolivia and Salvador Allende's Marxist government in Chile. Most of the members of the student council were Communist, except me. I had always been fearless in my convictions, even at the price of mockery and ridicule. I was the opposite of what they were. I was pro-American, democratic, and a pacifist. They did not like me.

One day at a student rally I spoke in favor of the Peace Corps, which my audience thought was a group of "Yankee imperialist agents." My comments were not well taken. After the rally, I was surrounded by an angry mob that wanted to lynch me. I was shoved, pushed, tossed, and was about to be beaten. I thought I was going to die that day. But out of nowhere, there appeared a tall man with a backpack. I had never seen him before. He was not a student. He grabbed me by my shirt and pulled me out of the angry mob. He saved my life. At the time I thought he was a CIA agent. I now think he was an angel. I never saw him again.

At the time I also did not know God. I did not deserve to be rescued that day, but I was. I am baffled and humbled that God would even want to rescue me. Yet He loved me enough before I even knew Him to send an angel after me.

He Chose Us to Live the Abundant Life

The gospel tells us that even when we were weak and did not know Him, "God so loved the world that he gave his one and only Son, that whoever believes in him shall not perish but have eternal life" (John 3:16).

It is truly amazing and astonishing that God would intervene in our lives, and yet He does. What are we to Him? Job asked this question of God. "What is man that you make so much of him, that you give him so much attention, that you examine him every morning and test him every moment?" (Job 7:17–18).

All He asks is that we believe. Through belief we are saved, strengthened, and rescued. He renews our strength and gives power to the weak. He enables us to finish the race.

CHAPTER 10
CHOOSE LIFE OVER DEATH

She was barely eighteen years old and in the first semester of college when she became pregnant. Her boyfriend, whom she barely knew, wanted her to abort the pregnancy. She refused. He rejected her throughout her complicated pregnancy. She had to drop out of school and go on bed rest. She gave birth to a premature child who needed surgery soon after birth.

This young woman chose life, in spite of all its difficulties. God rewarded her choice. That child is the joy of her life.

Like her, many women worldwide face pregnancy without the love and support of their partners or their families. They struggle with the choices of life and death. Regrettably, some choose to end their pregnancies. They choose death.

Reverence for Life

As followers of Christ, we must recognize the sanctity of human life and have reverence for it. Human life is God's gift. It belongs to Him. He gives life, and He takes it away. It is not ours; it does not belong to us. "A man's life is not his own" (Jeremiah 10:23). We cannot give it, nor can we take it away. This point has been said so many times in the years since the Supreme Court's decision to legalize abortion that it sounds like an old cliché. But it is actually still relevant and applicable to many issues surrounding human life that are controversial in our society today.

The complexity of life and death decisions in our culture at present makes it easy for people to become confused and get caught up in deceptive philosophies and their worldly principles. One of these principles says if it is pleasurable, do it. Another says if it bothers, get rid of it. Both are part of a deceptive philosophy that says life on earth is the result of human actions, and it begins at birth, not conception. If a person accepts this philosophy as the truth, then it becomes acceptable to abort a pregnancy as well as to destroy an embryo to obtain stem cells for research.

Some argue that embryonic stem cell research furthers the common good and is therefore permissible. They state that the common good trumps what others might think. At issue here is whether it is acceptable to destroy a life in order to prolong the life of others; essentially, whether the ends justify the means.

Still others argue that there needs to be exceptions to the sanctity of all human life principle. They would allow abortions for genetically abnormal pregnancies, babies with serious birth defects, and pregnancies that are the result of rape or incest. At the heart of each of these issues are two opposing philosophies. One upholds the sanctity of human life without exceptions. The other allows exceptions for various reasons. The exceptions change from time to time, and are therefore man-made rules.

God's rules never change; they are clear and categorical. The Bible says, "You should not murder" (Exodus 20:13). As a physician and a Christian, I understand that command to mean all human life, in all circumstances. It refers to the young and the old, the born and the unborn, the embryonic and the developed, the criminal and the just, the sinful and the pure.

As followers of Christ, you and I must be clear on the issues and uphold life. Our stand on life and death choices and our reverence for all life can help others who are confused by the world's philosophies to find the answers they seek and to choose life.

Earthly Life and Eternal Life

A far greater issue than any of these earthly life choices is the matter of eternal life.

God loved us so much that He sent Jesus to earth to make the choice clear: eternal life with Him, or death and damnation for all of eternity. John 17:3 says, "Now this is eternal life: that they may know you, the only true God, and Jesus Christ, whom you have sent."

Scripture teaches that we were dead in our sins and in our transgressions, but through faith in Jesus Christ, we have eternal life. So great is the Father's love that through Him we have passed from death to life (see 1 John 3:14).

Life on earth is a work in progress. It is a process of being progressively molded into the image of God's Son with certainty that God will complete what He has started in us. The apostle Paul tells the Christians in Philippi of his confidence that "he who began a good work in you will carry it on to completion until the day of Christ Jesus" (Philippians 1:6).

Life on earth is also a process of purification, of becoming more and more like Christ. Romans 8:29 states that "those God foreknew he also predestined to be conformed in the likeness of his Son, that he may be the firstborn among many brothers." Becoming more like Jesus should be the correct focus of our life so that we work for things eternal and not for things that perish.

All life on earth is a gift from God, and so is eternal life with Him in heaven. We must see earthly life as a mission and a task that we must complete without regrets or complaints and with great courage. We must trust that God will provide the necessary tools to see the mission successfully accomplished, and we must be confident in the ultimate outcome, eternal life with Him.

God Chose Us

From the beginning of the world, God knew those who would accept His message. We must believe in the promises of God that state that we were chosen of God to do good works, that He will see us through all the difficulties of our life, that He will use those difficulties to mold us and shape us into the likeness of His Son, and that He will turn evil circumstances into good. God did not promise that there would be no difficulties in our life, but that He would be there with us and work for our good when we face difficulties.

It is essential that our lives reflect these promises. Our lives must reflect our acceptance of God's plan of salvation so that when all is said and done, our life's story shows that we were purified by righteousness, that our choices transformed us into the likeness of God's Son, and that we chose life over death in all occasions and under all circumstances.

Life and Death in the Amazon Jungle of Peru

The Amazon Jungle of Peru is both a place of immense pristine beauty and also a place of brutal and savage reality, where every day the issues of life and death unfold in the delicate balance of nature. There the survival of an animal species depends on its predatory capacity upon another while being simultaneously subjected to predation.

The Indian tribes of the Amazon understand this delicate balance. During their lifetime Indian women are frequently pregnant, giving birth to as many as ten to twelve offspring. Due to the harsh realities of life in the jungle, only half survive childhood. Childbirth itself is full of perils. The level of healthcare is dismal. Deliveries are attended by unskilled birth attendants, and when complications happen, there are no easily accessible resources to meet the emergency.

Even though the government of Peru has established a sparse network of health clinics in the jungle, these clinics are not easily accessible and are frequently understaffed and underfunded. These clinics also suffer from unreliable water and electrical supply and a tenuous supply chain of basic medical equipment.

Travel in the jungle is filled with perils, including washed away dirt roads with car-size potholes and boats that break down in desolate areas of the many rivers of the Amazon basin. To these perils add the risks of malaria, yellow fever, TB, and rabies. This last one is transmitted by bat bites that occur while a person is sleeping. There are also poisonous spiders, which can be as large as the palm of a hand, and numerous poisonous snakes. Other dangers include armed robbery by gunmen that operate in remote roads and murders committed by Shining Path Communist guerrillas in the name of political grandstanding.

In the midst of this darkness stands the church of Jesus Christ, like a flower that springs up in the muddy swamps of the great Amazon River. The Church of the Nazarene has had a fifty-year presence there. Larry and Adie Garman are missionaries there, and they have been largely responsible for bringing the gospel to the Aguaruna Indian tribe. This tribe is composed of approximately 60,000 people. Around 10,000 are now Christians.

I have listened to the Garmans' testimonies numerous times, both in the jungle and at our church in West Chester, Ohio. At the beginning of their ministry, there were very few conversions. It was like planting a seed in very dry soil that yields little fruit. Being persistent and steadfast, the Garmans continued their ministry. Despite their initial disappointment, God rewarded their efforts. They have seen an abundant harvest of souls in their thirty-six plus years in that nation.

My church, the West Chester Church of the Nazarene, has partnered with the Garmans in their ministry. For many years it has sent work and witness teams to the Amazon to build new church buildings, build structures for the Nazarene Bible Institute, and do repair work at the mission station of Nuevo Horizonte (New Horizon). Of the three hundred church buildings of the Nazarene denomination now standing in the Amazon Jungle of Peru, at least twelve have been built by members of my church, including one in honor of my parents in the village of Teneshtum, a short distance from Nuevo Horizonte.

To reach these underserved women of the Amazon Jungle of Peru was the primary motivation of the two medical missions I have made to that region of the world so far. Both trips were a mixture of humanitarian intent and a motivation to bring the gospel of Jesus Christ to all the corners of the earth. For each trip, preparations were analogous to stocking and bringing a complete field hospital there. The team brought supplies and equipment to meet all conceivable emergencies that might have arisen in the course of doing surgery there.

Bringing the Light of Life

On my second trip there, news of the arrival of the medical team spread like wildfire in the jungle. People walked for days to reach Nuevo Horizonte. Patients camped out on the grounds of the mission station.

We arrived after dark, around 10 p.m. local time, after traveling sixteen hours by bus from the City of Chiclayo, across the Andes Mountains, and into the jungle. We were greeted with the most beautiful welcoming hymns, sung in Aguaruno language, by the students at the Nazarene Bible Institute. Their voices were a soothing balm after a long, harrowing day. These students were praising God and thanking Him for sending a medical team to help their people.

I will never forget the faces of the patients, which spoke of long suffering and a lifetime of waiting for someone to come to help relieve their suffering. Their pain and their suffering left a permanent mark on my soul. I remember four women with advanced cervical cancer. For them we could do nothing medically except to offer pain relief, our solidarity, and the love and comfort of Jesus. There were also women whose uterus had dropped due to their numerous deliveries. These women had suffered for many years without hope of having corrective surgery. And there were also many men and women with large abdominal hernias caused by a lifetime of carrying heavy loads.

We operated on the ones we could at the New Horizon mission station in an improvised operating room, using house lights as our only light source. After surgery, we placed the patients on bamboo cots set up in an adjacent room. We hung their IV fluid bags on nails pounded into the wooden walls.

The ones needing more extensive surgery were separated from the main group and taken in minibuses to the regional hospital in the city of Bagua, which was six hours away. With permission from the hospital director there, we performed hysterectomies and other abdominal surgeries.

As the time for our departure grew near, we bid farewell to our patients, praying over them for God to complete their recovery and to direct their paths for the rest of their lives. Their task, like ours, was to fulfill the mission that God had ordained for this life.

The Choice for Life

This chapter is not meant to judge, shame, stir up, or assign guilt but to offer the love and comfort of the Father to all who need it. We are not Christians because we are perfect. Far from it! We are Christians because we are forgiven in spite of our wrong choices.

It is through grace that we are saved. We are not saved by our own merits or our own perfection, because we all have weaknesses and imperfections. We are saved and made whole through repentance and God's forgiveness. "Godly sorrow brings repentance that leads to salvation" (2 Corinthians 7:10). Salvation, in turn, leads us into abundant life here and eternal life to come.

The choice for life as Christ's disciple is an active choice, one that demands our active involvement, requiring us to take risks and to give our very best and our very all. It is a choice that impacts our human life like no other choice; more importantly, it impacts our eternal life. We must not fail to choose life and help others do so too.

CHAPTER 11
CHOOSE PEACE OVER STRIFE

Peace on earth is God's original plan, His vision for all humanity. Conflict, strife, and war are our own doing, the result of our failures.

Enduring peace requires our active involvement. It is the result of arduous work. We are in the world not as passive observers, but as active participants. We are "to seek peace and pursue it" (Psalm 34:14).

The quest for peace is based on mutual respect and understanding as well as on mutual benefit. The process of building up one another goes beyond the Golden Rule; it calls us to esteem others more highly than ourselves to the point of self-sacrifice, expecting nothing in return. This principle applies to our personal life, and it is equally applicable to the foreign policy of our nation. Certainly the world would be a better place if all people and governments adhered to this principle.

Peace and Social Justice

Peace is based on social justice. There cannot be lasting peace when social injustice prevails. Injustice, unfairness, and inequity are at the roots of strife. If we want a lasting peace, we must address these root causes and devote our efforts to solve the problems they perpetuate. Without a doubt, the greatest of these problems is poverty.

Some say eliminating poverty is a mission for government agencies and international relief organizations. They believe that individual efforts can do next to nothing to change a problem of this magnitude. The truth is that poverty will persist and remain unsolved until we all become involved for the long term. Government and relief programs alone are unable to cope with the problem.

Taking Care of the Poor

A litmus test of true Christianity is how we take care of the poor. In other words, we cannot claim to have a relationship with the Father and not take care of the poor.

The Bible contains numerous passages on taking care of the poor. Deuteronomy 15:7–8 states: "Do not be hardhearted or tightfisted toward your poor brother. Rather be openhanded." Many blessings are provided to those who take care of the weak and the poor. "Blessed is he who has regard for the weak; the Lord delivers him in times of trouble" (Psalm 41:1). There are also rebukes for those who fail to do so. "He who oppresses the poor shows contempt for their Maker, but whoever is kind to the needy honors God" (Proverbs 14:31). It is obvious that God has special concern for the poor.

Amos, God's prophet, was a humble shepherd. The people of Israel had become complacent in their status and comfort, all the while oppressing the poor and ignoring their needs. God gave Amos a vision of His judgment for Israel to share with the people. "This is what the Lord says: 'For three sins of Israel, even for four, I will not turn back my wrath. They sell the righteous for silver, and the needy for a pair of sandals. They trample on the heads of the poor as upon the dust of the ground and deny justice to the oppressed" (Amos 2:6–7). God then sent destruction upon Israel: a powerful earthquake took place two years later, and thirty years later, the nation was conquered by the Assyrian Empire (722 BC).

The gospel of Luke describes how Jesus at the beginning of His earthly ministry gave the Sermon on the Mount, in which He clearly explained His philosophy on the poor. Contrary to the prevailing thinking of His time in which riches were seen as signs of God's favor, Jesus emphatically declared that God's favor rests with the poor.

"Blessed are you who are poor, for yours is the kingdom of God. Blessed are you who hunger now, for you will be satisfied" (Luke 6:20–21).

Advocacy for the poor must go beyond verbal statements of sympathy; it must include actions that reverse the injustices that the world inflicts upon the poor. "Woe to those who make unjust laws, to those who issue oppressive decrees, to deprive the poor of their rights" (Isaiah 10:1–2).

"Take care" is an action statement. It applies to here and now, today. It does not refer to a time in the future when we have the means, if we win the lotto, or when we retire.

In the gospel of Matthew is recorded the story of the rich young man who told Jesus he was perfect in following all the requirements of the law. "'All these I have kept,' the young man said. 'What do I still lack?' Jesus answered, 'If you want to be perfect, go, sell your possessions and give to the poor'" (Matthew 19:20–21). In other words, we miss the point of our salvation if we do not take care of the poor.

The largest issue of poverty is hunger. It is the first one to address in our quest to have lasting peace with other nations. A flagrant paradox of our times is that the world now produces enough food to feed every human being on the planet (www.worldhunger.org). Despite this fact, hunger and its companions, malnutrition and disease, are still rampant in the third world. It is shocking that wealthy governments and societies destroy their crops and pay their farmers not to plant in order to keep up crop prices rather than find ways to donate their surplus to those who need it. It seems not only uncaring and unfair but also almost criminal in light of the need for food all over the world.

The lie says we can do next to nothing to help solve the problem of hunger in the world. The truth says we are to "take care of" the poor. The solution begins today by giving a portion of our resources to feed those who are hungry. The opportunities and the options are amazingly easy to find. Our individual actions to feed the hungry and take care of the poor are part of our choice of peace over strife.

Overcoming Evil with Good

To live in harmony with others in the world, we must address other injustices besides hunger, which is only a part of poverty. Another basic biblical principle that we must begin to apply actively to work for peace states that we must not repay evil with evil. Romans 12:21 says, "Do not be overcome by evil, but overcome evil with good."

We must be willing to face evil and go beyond it. We must forgive, not take revenge, but we must also give unmerited favor. "If your enemy is hungry, feed him; if he is thirsty, give him something to drink" (Romans 12:20). It may seem like a difficult principle to accept, especially in the face of terrorist attacks, but it is one we must master if we want lasting peace.

In Papua New Guinea, until very recently, the only socially acceptable response to personal injury or loss of life or livelihood was retaliation. Any such matter automatically fell under tribal jurisdiction, which often resulted in onerous conditions being placed upon another tribe. These conditions had all the necessary ingredients for creating a perfect environment for violence. Not surprisingly, tribal warfare was, and still is, common and prevalent.

With the advent of Christianity and the acceptance of the Christian doctrine of forgiveness there, the need for repayment of evil with evil has become less appealing and less necessary. The people of Papua New Guinea now rely on the remedies that the legal system provides and now enjoy a measure of peace that has been brought about by their renunciation of the social norm of repayment of evil with evil. It is now possible and permissible to repay evil with good.

Personal Sacrifice

Peace requires our own personal sacrifice and suffering. We all like the gospel of prosperity. We all want God to enlarge our physical territory and to prosper us, as stated in the prayer of Jabez (see 1

Chronicles 4). However, few people accept the gospel of sacrifice and suffering. Enlarging our spiritual territory and increasing the fruitfulness of our righteousness can require profound sacrifice and suffering. Look at the example of the apostle Paul, who was stoned, flogged, shipwrecked, and finally martyred for the gospel when God enlarged his territory to be an apostle to the Gentiles.

The choice of peace that leads to abundant life for us begins when we personally give up some of our comfort and prosperity so that others may have it too. Peace on earth is advanced when all men and women of good will, who love the Lord, take up the cause of the poor and disenfranchised, the hungry and thirsty, the homeless and the sick. We are not to sit idly, but to work hard for social justice.

As in all choices of abundant life, Jesus is our example.

Personal Encounters with Poverty

I am absolutely convinced that there will be no peace on earth until the problem of poverty is addressed in a comprehensive manner that allows the four billion people of the world living on less than four dollars per day (www.worldbank.org) to achieve a level of development that narrows the gap with people living in more developed countries. The following narrative of my first medical mission to the Amazon Jungle of Peru presents my testimony on how God opened my eyes to the problem of poverty.

I was in for many surprises as I traveled with a medical team in metal boats with outboard engines down the Marañòn River. Our destination was the village of Nieva in the heart of the Amazon Jungle of Peru. The four-hour boat trip from the Nuevo Horizonte (New Horizon) mission station had taken us past Aquaruna Indians paddling in wooden canoes made out of hollowed tree trunks. As we traveled, we passed numerous Indian villages that were no more than a group of huts with straw roofs and adobe walls. Some of the larger villages had a wooden building with a tin roof that stood prominently at the center of the village. From the river, with the help of binoculars, we could see a yellow sign with three crosses posted on each of these buildings. It read: "Iglesia Del Nazareno" (Church of the Nazarene). These churches had, for the most part, been built over the years by work-and-witness mission teams from the United States.

The process of building a church in the jungle follows the following pattern with few exceptions: purchase of construction materials with project money from each team and placement of these materials at the construction site several months in advance; preparation of the site; establishment of a carpentry shop upon the team's arrival so that an electric saw powered by a gasoline generator can be used for cutting wooden planks; fabrication of the frame, placement of walls and a tin roof; and finally, dedication of the building to God upon completion of the project.

As we disembarked at the village of our team's destination, the muddy trail took us past dilapidated buildings with crumbling walls and rusted tin roofs. We walked on past a similarly rusted metal flagpole that displayed a very faded Peruvian flag. I could not help but notice the poverty that those run-down buildings demonstrated. The faded flag stood in my mind as a symbol of the presence of a government with few resources. But these were only pale reflections of the profound and deep-seated poverty of the people. They were barefoot, with few clothes to wear. Showing through their scant clothing were their emaciated bodies and bloated stomachs. Their smiles revealed significant tooth decay.

Instantly I was embarrassed by our wealth. We were well fed, had suitcases full of clothes, and were wearing hats and sunglasses, hiking boots and suntan lotion with insect repellent. The contrast was humbling, staggering, striking, and dramatic.

Our team was composed of many members, each with a different function. It reflected the biblical description of the body of Christ. The majority set out to work on the construction project, while my wife, Carol, and I went to work at the local health clinic.

Our surprises rapidly mounted: no running water, electricity for only a few hours of the day, a broken down exam table, no linen to cover the patients, first-time pelvic exams on adult Indian women done with flashlights, and the finding of several women with advanced cervical cancer. We were also challenged by patients with exotic medical conditions such as blindness caused by viral eye infections, children and adults with birth defects, and a boy dying with rabies caused by an infected bat bite. Even more challenging was the lack of medical resources and equipment to meet these needs. It seemed to us a medical nightmare.

Until then I had assumed that caring for the poor was largely a responsibility of government. To my surprise, government was, for the most part, unable to cope with the needs. In a very convincing manner, this mission to the Amazon Jungle of Peru revealed the intimate association between poverty and health and between social justice and peace; it also highlighted our responsibility for the poor and government's incapacity.

The world's poor are still waiting for a measure of social justice that will bring peace to earth. Those of us who long for peace must be committed to solving the problem of poverty, because it requires every one of us.

Personal Peace

Our efforts to promote peace result in a sense of satisfaction, a sense of a job well done, and of a mission accomplished. When we see the fruit of our efforts, we will know that we have worked for a purpose that is bigger than ourselves—not for our personal benefit or advancement, but for others. Personal peace, however, comes from a different source than our outward actions.

Personal peace comes from knowing God and having a relationship with Him. It is true for everyone on earth. In Him we can rest secure. As stated in Isaiah 32:17, "The fruit of righteousness will be peace."

Personal peace is not something we can work to achieve. Instead, it is wholly the work of the Spirit. When we are in God's will, the Spirit of God lives in us. We have a peace that transcends all understanding. No trial or tribulation, no challenge or sickness, no outcome or outlook can take away the peace within us that comes from the Spirit. "The mind controlled by the Spirit is life and peace" (Romans 8:6). Our personal peace is not bound by circumstances, and therefore we can have peace with our circumstances, whatever they are.

Live a Life of Peace

Peace is the fruit of a right relationship with God. Peace with others comes as a consequence of that. We are to live in peace with ourselves, with God, and with others.

We are to promote, protect, and advance the cause of peace. We are to seek and pursue it, laboring to bring up those who are downtrodden, downhearted, and discouraged. We are to be peacemakers instead of conflict makers, giving of ourselves sacrificially. Then our life on earth will be abundant. "Blessed are the peacemakers, for they will be called sons of God" (Matthew 5:9).

CHAPTER 12
CHOOSE COURAGE OVER FEAR

Fear is a natural, human response to life's dangers and troubles. It can serve as a simple warning for us to proceed with caution, but it can also cripple us. To live the life God intends, we need courage to overcome our fears. Courage is mental or moral strength. Author Ernest Hemingway defined it as grace under pressure (*Ernest Hemingway Selected Letters*, 199–201). I call it peace under fire.

Courage is peace under fire because it allows us to accomplish things that we would otherwise not be able to accomplish. In times of crisis, angst, and tribulation, we can have this quiet moral and spiritual strength that comes from God called courage.

God Gives Us Courage

Courage is the strength of the woman in labor and of the soldier who places himself in harm's way to protect his comrades. It allows them to do things they normally would not be able to do and to make personal sacrifices for the common good. Scripture promises that those whose trust is upon the Lord will be brave and courageous in times of trouble, while those whose trust is upon themselves alone for deliverance will see their knees buckle under pressure. "Be strong and courageous. Do not be afraid or terrified … for the Lord your God goes with you; he will never leave you nor forsake you" (Deuteronomy 31:6).

Courageous people will stand up to life's tests, but those who lack courage will be overcome by fear. Deborah, courageous judge of Israel, went into battle and won the victory when the warrior she commanded to go was unable to go alone because of fear (see Judges 4).

Fear: Satan's Weapon

Fear is not from God but from Satan. Fear has to do with punishment (see 1 John 4:18), and it is Satan's weapon. Therefore, whenever we have fear, we must recognize its origin and cast it away immediately.

The gospel is abundantly clear in stating that we, followers of Christ, must not be afraid. The sentence "do not be afraid" is one that is repeated over and over in the gospel. We first read these words in the Bible in the book of Genesis, as God is teaching Abraham what it means to live by faith. "The word of the Lord came to Abram in a vision, 'Do not be afraid, Abram'" (Genesis 15:1). We see these words again at the end of the Bible in the book of Revelation, when God gave John a vision of the end of the times. "When I saw him, I fell at his feet as though dead. Then he placed his right hand on me and said: 'Do not be afraid'" (Revelation 1:17). In between Genesis and Revelation, the Bible's pages are filled with examples of God's command to not be afraid.

The reason for God's command not to be afraid is that fear will immobilize us, incapacitate us, and render us ineffective. Because of fear, we will not attempt to do great things in His name, speak out boldly for those who have no voice, or take great risks. Instead, we will be settled and content in our own incapacity.

As alluded to previously, Deborah's story is one of courage based on trust in God, with the conviction that God prepares the way for those to whom He has assigned a task to do. In contrast, the story of her commanding officer, Barak, is one of fear of failure due to trust in his own abilities and not trust in God.

Fear of failure is one kind of fear that keeps us from becoming better and greater; it keeps us from attempting new endeavors and from learning new skills. In essence, we cannot reach the summit of the mountain unless we give up our fear of heights.

Fear of ridicule is another kind of fear that debilitates. Fear of ridicule gives the crowds an importance they do not deserve. It bows down to their wishes and makes us hostage to their directives. Others' opinions of us should not rule our lives. Our confidence is not in others, but in Him who lives in us.

God in Us: the Hope of Glory

The story of Hezekiah, king of the small nation of Israel, is told in 2 Chronicles 31–32. Hezekiah did what was "good and right and faithful before the Lord" (2 Chronicles 31:20). As he faced what seemed an almost assured defeat before a more powerful enemy, he was diligent in preparing his city and his people for battle. He encouraged them with these words: "Be strong and courageous. Do not be afraid or discouraged … for there is a greater power with us than with him" (2 Chronicles 32:7). Hezekiah's courage came from his absolute confidence that God was with them.

Courage, in contrast to fear, allows us to complete our tasks; it allows us to be fruitful and effective. The good news of the gospel is that we are forgiven; as forgiven people, Christ lives in us, and the power of His Spirit is ours. Because He lives in us, we can attempt great things. He gives us the courage we need for every circumstance. Jesus said, "Do not be afraid. Take courage, for I have overcome the world" (John 16:33, author's paraphrase). When we stand in the truth and in the light, God is with us, and the world cannot overcome us.

Because He gives us courage, we can go to the ends of the earth and not be afraid; we can tackle a difficult project and find solutions to its problems; we can stand up for what is right, even when no one else shares our views.

Courage is born of God's love, and nothing on earth is greater than His love. "Your love, O Lord, reaches to the heavens, your faithfulness to the skies" (Psalm 36:5). God's love enables us to stand in full confidence and not to fear tomorrow. "Perfect love drives out fear" (1 John 4:18).

My Patients' Courage

Throughout my medical career I have been blessed by my patients in many ways. They have given significance to my life, giving me a purpose and a calling. They have allowed me to share in their joys and in their sorrows. Through them I have experienced the glory of success when their health is improved or restored and also the agony of defeat when all efforts are exhausted and we have reached the end of the road.

I have come to admire many qualities in my patients, but the one that stands out above the rest is courage. In so many, there is a quiet fortitude that allows them to continue on despite their suffering and their sickness, accepting what is inevitable without complaining. There is a confidence in them in the final outcome and a certainty about their destiny, no matter what their circumstances.

Some of them have cancer. Happily, today cancer is not a death sentence, for at least half are long-term survivors, and many lead productive lives while still living with the disease. Unfortunately, some reach terminal stage despite best efforts. I see their faces and the dignified manner with which they go through their treatment, which in many cases involves surgery, radiation therapy, and chemotherapy. When the disease can't be halted, their ravaged bodies show the effects. But their spirits remained strong, unfazed, and untouched, exuding that quiet strength that we call courage.

There is courage also in the mother whose child has died and also in the child who is terminally ill. "God was good to me yesterday when I gave birth to my son, and He is still good today," said a young mother at her child's funeral. With trust in God and with great courage, she then said her final good-byes.

The Meaning of Suffering

Suffering is inextricably intertwined and woven into our human nature; it is part of the substance of life. Even when we are leading right and blameless lives, suffering will eventually come knocking at our doors. Sooner or later we all have to endure it.

Suffering can be a great teacher as long as we have courage and choose the correct attitude. Our attitude about the experience of suffering determines whether we profit or are crushed by it.

Let me be clear: suffering is not necessary for growth, and it should be avoided or alleviated whenever possible. Nevertheless, sometimes suffering is inescapable.

The Word tells us what the profitable outcomes of inescapable suffering are. Romans 5:3–4 states, "We also rejoice in our sufferings, because we know that suffering produces perseverance; perseverance, character; and character, hope." Stated simply, suffering further defines and molds our character.

Suffering refocuses our attention from the false promise of our earthly comfort and security and places our attention where it rightfully belongs—on God. In his book, *The Problem of Pain* (Harper Collins, 2001), C.S. Lewis states that pain and suffering is God's megaphone. Sometimes we do not hear God when He whispers and things are well. Our hearing is muffled and hampered by the noise of the world. When we suffer, God raises His voice above the clamor of our life in order to be heard. Pain and suffering wake us up from our stupor of comfort and security.

Suffering is not only a part of life, but it is also our destiny as believers. "For it has been granted to you on behalf of Christ not only to believe on him, but also to suffer for him" (Philippians 1:29). The gospel clearly states that all Christians should be ready to suffer because of their faith. In fact, many Christians living in non-Christian countries do.

The Christian Church under Communism

The 1960 revolution that ushered Communism into Cuba marked the beginning of thirty years of discrimination and punishment for Christians there. A Christian brother of mine gave me his testimony about his life as a Christian in Cuba to share here. He asked that I withhold his name for fear of retribution.

During those years, Christianity was frowned upon and discouraged by the ruling authorities. Christians who openly professed their faith were denied jobs and access to higher education. Questions about faith and religious affiliation were asked on all application forms; only forms with negative responses were acted upon.

Bibles were confiscated and destroyed as subversive material. My friend described an incident during the 1960s where thousands of Bibles were burned in the public square in Havana. The revolution viewed Christianity as an "ideological problem" that required "ideological reeducation." Despite its suffering, however, the Christian church persevered.

During the 1990s, it became politically expedient for the regime, realizing it could not prevail, to relax its rules gradually. Religious activities were progressively tolerated. After those thirty years of Communist indoctrination that proclaimed the death of God, Cubans were hungry for Jesus and ripe for the gospel. Christianity experienced an explosive growth.

There is now an improved environment for worship in Cuba; the government has reexamined its religious policy to the point that in 2009, the Gideons were granted permission to legally introduce one million Bibles into the country.

The people of Cuba still suffer under an oppressive regime that profoundly curtails their freedom, but for the time being, there is significant progress in the freedom of religious expression. Praise be to God!

Even though we can expect suffering in our lives, we who are Christians can always count on having the presence of our Lord to carry us through it. We are not alone in our suffering.

Not All Have Courage

Unfortunately, not all of my patients exhibit courage when facing suffering. Some are gripped by fear. They fear losing control over their lives; they fear illness and death; they also fear judgment.

Here I have great opportunities for ministry. It is a time when God has their undivided attention, and I can be an instrument of His. I have found that one does not need special credentials to be a witness for God, to present God's plan for salvation, or to be an instrument in His hand. All He needs is our willingness. He takes away our fear of not being well received or of being perceived as unscientific. We plant the seed, and God takes care of the rest.

I recall a young woman who had undergone surgery for cervical cancer, and her boyfriend and she wanted guaranties that she had been cured. I responded cautiously and stated that time would tell. We would know if she was cured when her pap smears became normal and remained normal over time. They, however, wanted to know immediately. I told them that it was a good time for prayer. This statement was not well received. The young woman left my practice because she thought that I was unscientific. She acted out of fear of losing control of her life and not allowing God any room to take control.

Happily, most patients are receptive to the same message I gave her and are glad that their physician is a doctor of the soul as well as of the body.

The Orphans' Courage

I have not seen a greater display of courage than that exhibited by the orphans of the HIV/AIDS epidemic in Africa. Children orphaned of their parents face unbelievable and unimaginable challenges every day. They demonstrate courage in many ways, overcoming the threats of their harsh environment: disease, hunger, dirty water, and other human beings. The following narrative illustrates their plight, and is also a testimony to their courage. It is an eyewitness account I wrote after visiting a location for orphans on a mission trip to Swaziland in 2008.

> Many are not going to make it. The odds are stacked up against them. They live precarious existences. In dilapidated dwellings, with hardly any clothing, barefoot, and barely surviving, they are the orphans of the HIV/AIDS epidemic in Africa.
> They live in thatched roof huts with mud walls and an earthen floor. They have few furnishings and no running water, sewage disposal, or electricity. The children sleep on straw mats on the floor. There is a separate hut for cooking meals, which are cooked by burning wood. This hut has an opening at the rooftop to allow some of the smoke to escape. In spite of this, the hut is smoky and unhealthy. The children eat only once a day, a diet of corn porridge and beans. A third building on the premises is an outhouse. This structure has a rooftop, walls, and a hole on the ground without a cover.
> At least two hours of every day are devoted to getting water. They get it from a well located several miles away. They carry it in 20-liter plastic containers. These dirty and heavy containers are carried back to their huts by balancing them on top of their heads or on wheelbarrows.
> The water from the well is now clean. Before World Vision drilled the well, water was obtained from a dirty pond many more miles away, where animals drink, bathe, place their droppings, and die. Their carcasses then rot in the sun and contaminate the water.
> At age nine, he looks like a six-year-old. Due to malnutrition, his growth is stunted. Thin and squalid, he has few smiles, and one can sense that his spirit is crushed. Lacking self-esteem, he has no eye contact, is shy and inexpressive. He is barefoot. His shirt is torn and has many holes.

Both his parents died after falling ill. In Africa, there is still great stigma and shame associated with HIV/AIDS, and it is considered impolite to ask their cause of death. He will only say that they were chronically ill. They were buried on the family plot, a place too painful to share with visitors.

He is being raised by his ninety-year-old grandmother. He is one of the lucky ones. He is attending school thanks to a sponsorship from World Vision that pays for his school fees, uniforms, and health clinic visits when needed. A food supplement is also provided once a month.

Others are not so fortunate. While they are still children, the oldest ones become head of the house once their parents die. They are left with the responsibility of looking after their younger siblings. They are robbed not only of the love and comfort of their parents, but also of their childhood and their dreams. Their plight is so desperate as to soften the hardest heart. Regrettably, this is not an isolated event, as there are countless children-headed households in Africa.

They do survive, however, thanks to community and church volunteers who look after them as well as those chronically ill with HIV. They receive regular home visits, food rations and help with basic needs.

Some orphans live in orphanages run by faith-based organizations, while others attend soup kitchens. There they receive one meal a day—just enough to stay alive.

There is a noticeable generation gap in Africa with a generation clearly missing. One can only see the very young or the very old, with a big gap of middle-aged people. They have succumbed to tuberculosis and AIDS. In Africa, most AIDS deaths are from TB, as victims are unable to fight TB due to their immune suppression.

Most of the three million yearly AIDS deaths worldwide are in sub-Sahara Africa. Children are most vulnerable to malaria, accounting for the majority of their one million yearly deaths.

Poverty and hunger are the other necessary ingredients that fan the fires of illness and death in Africa.

One third of the citizens of the world live in extreme poverty, defined by the United Nations as living on less than one dollar per day (www.worldbank.org). Faith-based organizations such as World Vision are at the forefront of the fight against poverty and hunger. They are starting to turn the tide of despair and early death.

World Vision's mission statement says it is a Christian relief and development organization devoted to saving the children by addressing the causes of hunger. Founded by Reverend Robert Pierce, it operates primarily in rural areas, rather than urban areas, in poor countries of the third world. It works through a network of orphan and vulnerable children sponsorships, community partnerships, and area development projects. Area Development Programs (ADPs) begin with a survey of needs and identifications of orphans and vulnerable children (OVCS) as well as those that are chronically ill. Then there is community response team development with volunteers for home visits to address needs. In addition, sustainable development projects are established for growing crops and animal husbandry, clean water projects, and water management schemes. All these programs emphasize self-reliance and empowerment, discouraging a culture of dependency.

Africa has already lost a generation to HIV/AIDS, and it is at risk of also losing the next generation to drought, hunger, and water-borne illnesses. Unless we act now in a bold and decisive manner, many orphans and vulnerable children are not going to make it. It is imperative that we act now. There is no time to lose. We have only one life, and we have to do something!

I urge you to sponsor a child, to involve yourself and your church in community partnership projects, to pray for Africa, to go to Africa.

God is up to something when we see the number of people visiting Africa to work, to bear witness, and to help bear their burdens; but it is only a drop in the bucket, and more workers and help are needed. God is up to something when ordinary people, such as you and me, can make an investment in the lives of others and leave a legacy that transcends our human lives. God is up to something when, as Robert Pierce once said, our hearts can be broken by the things that break the heart of God.

(This article was originally published in my guest column in the *Hamilton Journal News*—a daily news journal published in Hamilton, Ohio—on April 28, 2008.)

God has given us a spirit of power and not a spirit of timidity (see 2 Timothy 1:7). Regardless of our circumstances, God provides the courage necessary to overcome the challenges we face in life. These challenges do not compare to the ones faced by the orphans of the HIV/AIDS epidemic. Their courage is truly inspirational and exemplary.

The choice of courage is rooted in our trust in God, who enables us to complete the tasks assigned to us. The choice of fear arises from dependence on our limited abilities and, in essence, represents distrust in God. It is our choice. What shall it be: courage or fear?

CHAPTER 13

CHOOSE THANKFULNESS OVER ANGER

A child is born by cesarean section. It is the culmination of a long and complicated pregnancy. The parents and their families have eagerly awaited this moment. It is, however, a bittersweet moment. Soon after birth, the adorable baby girl is in trouble. She turns blue, and it is obvious that she has difficulty breathing. She is rapidly rushed into the neonatal intensive care unit. It is discovered that she has a complex cardiac anomaly that will require immediate surgery just to stay alive. Months later, when she is stronger, she will need a heart transplant.

The parents, both in their twenties, are stunned and devastated. "Please say it ain't so," says the father as the mother bursts into tears. They had expected a perfect baby, even though the heart anomaly had been detected during the pregnancy. Their doctors had discussed extensively the seriousness of the condition, but deep inside they both had hoped that it was not true and that their child would be well.

They are facing an uncertain future, plagued with questions and anxiety. They also are experiencing conflicted feelings. On the one hand, they feel a twinge of anger and resentment, blaming God for allowing this complication to happen. On the other hand, they are thankful for their beautiful daughter. Having been raised in the church and being Christians, they understand and accept that God will provide for their needs, and they are thankful that they are not alone in this crisis.

Not All Are Thankful

But not everyone is thankful when the chips are down. Some are angry at God.

I recall another young family facing similar circumstances. Their child was also born with a complex cardiac anomaly requiring a heart transplant. The road ahead was certainly arduous and hard. The parents were overwhelmed with a sick child waiting for a donor. They were keenly distressed by the crude reality of needing somebody else's child to die in order for their boy to survive.

Their boy was placed on a national transplant waiting list. His condition was progressively deteriorating. Time was running out. Then, one night, the long-awaited call came in. "Get to the hospital right now. We have a donor's heart. It is being flown in." In another city, another family's boy had been killed in a motor vehicle accident.

The transplant surgery was long, difficult, and complicated. So was the post-operative course: threats of organ rejection, delayed wound healing, and a long hospital stay. The next few years were just as stressful and complicated: organ rejection, infections, and drug reactions. Somewhere along the way, this couple lost their faith. Their feelings could best be described as a mixture of anger against God and anger against the world. They came to believe that God was indifferent to their fate.

Many more years later, they experienced a change in heart. They enrolled their child, now seven years old, in a Christian school. They made overtures aimed at reviving their long-silenced faith, but have not regained it as of yet. They still do not attend church, but their child does, thanks to his grandparents.

Through the years, this couple focused on their anger at God instead of on seeing God's blessings. In their anger, they failed to see God's presence in every one of those hospital admissions; they also failed to see God's provisions, giving them the means to be able to take care of their sick child.

Anger Separates Us from God

In the face of difficult circumstances, some people, even Christians, do choose anger and resentment instead of thankfulness. These attitudes are not from God but from His adversary, Satan. They separate us from God and can lead us in a downward spiral that ends in spiritual death and darkness.

Anger displeases God and diminishes His reflection in our lives. "Man's anger does not bring about the righteous life that God desires" (James 1:20). It is extreme ingratitude, ignoring all that God has done for us. Anger is selfish and self-serving; it is about our desires and our egos. Anger and its companion, resentment, are destructive to the soul. We must not harbor anger in our hearts, where it can corrode and destroy the spirit.

Be Thankful Always

The Bible states in 1 Thessalonians 5:18, "Give thanks in all circumstances." In all circumstances means all of them, not only the good ones. Our natural tendency is to be thankful only in the good times. But we are to be thankful also in bad times. We are to be thankful for God's presence and His ability to carry us through tough times of crisis.

Some people are not thankful, even in good times when they are in full receipt of God's favor. They seem to think that their success is the fruit of their own effort only, and that they owe nothing to God. Their arrogance is crass and shameful in the light of God's goodness to them. "For from within, out of men's hearts, come evil thoughts ... arrogance and folly" (Mark 7:21–22).

I am reminded of the parable of the ten lepers that were healed, and only one came back to give thanks (see Luke 17:15–19). "Were not all ten cleansed? Where are the other nine?" (verse 17). It pleases God when we acknowledge His gifts and His favor, not taking them for granted.

A short list of often overlooked gifts from God reads something like this: our health and the perfect function of our bodies, our spouse and family, our jobs, our homes, our friends, and our church family. When we focus on His gifts and our abundance, there is no room for anger or resentment.

God does not need our gratitude. Our ingratitude actually hurts us, not Him, because we miss the opportunity to know more about God's character and nature and to enjoy the benefits of His grace.

He has given us much more than we ever deserved or imagined. He gave His only Son so that we could have eternal life. He paid the price for our salvation. Such knowledge must make us overwhelmingly thankful, and we can say, like the apostle Paul, "Thanks be to God for his indescribable gift!" (2 Corinthians 9:15). He also gave us the Holy Spirit and the gifts of the Holy Spirit. And Romans 8:35–39 says nothing can separate us from His love. He continues to loves us despite our imperfections and looks after us.

Expressing Thankfulness

We can express our thankfulness to God by saying thanks to Him quietly and privately, and we can also do so publicly and loudly. We can thank Him in every prayer, recognizing and acknowledging His gifts. But more than all of these expressions of thankfulness, we can thank Him most powerfully by living lives that are pleasing to Him. We can proclaim our gratitude by being a light in the darkness of this world.

The things that we do for Him, our good works, are outward expressions of our thanksgiving. The Bible says that our faith is made visible to the world in works that give glory to God (see James 2:17–22). They are not necessary for our salvation, but they are proofs of the good deposit that has been made in us. False faith, in contrast, has no works. "Faith by itself, if it is not accompanied by action, is dead" (James 2:17). False faith is a form of religion, but it is lifeless and expressionless. Those whose faith is false go through the motions of a religion but without conviction, without their hearts being in it.

I cannot emphasize enough the need for all Christians to demonstrate their thankfulness to God and their faith in Him through good works. They are the evidence and proof that we possess genuine faith and have received salvation.

Thankfulness and gratitude come from seeing our abundance. They are uplifting and encouraging emotions. Anger and resentment come from seeing what we do not have. They are negative feelings that plunge us into darkness. The choice is ours.

CHAPTER 14

CHOOSE BEING HEALED OVER BEING SICK

Most of us do not choose sickness. We try to maintain our health by making healthy decisions about our diet, exercise, avoidance of toxins such as tobacco and alcohol, and substance dependence. Some of us make poor choices in these areas and have to deal with the consequences of those poor choices. Yet despite our best efforts, the wonderful machine that is our body does break down, and we eventually and inevitably face illness.

Facing Illness

How we face illness in many ways determines the outcome. If we face it with fear and pessimism, we condition ourselves toward a poor outcome. If we face it with a positive, optimistic attitude, our chances of recovery, even from serious illness, are increased. Our mind exerts powerful influence over our body.

We can actually choose to be healed over being sick. That choice is not simply wishing health and sickness will go away. It is appealing to the source of all healing, God, and asking to be healed.

This statement may sound strange coming from a medical doctor trained in Western medicine. Doctors in this country are supposed to be scientific and logical. Today's medicine is evidence based. All treatments and decisions need to stand up to scrutiny and be proven by the scientific method. I fully endorse these principles, and yet some cases are exceptions to the rules and defy scientific logic.

The Choice Is Ours

I once had a patient whose story is an example. She was thirty-five-years old and had been diagnosed with advanced and incurable breast cancer. Her prognosis was poor. The treatments offered could not be curative anymore, but palliative—to prolong the quality and duration of her life, perhaps only by a few months.

I strongly believe in prayer as a powerful tool capable of changing the outcome in any situation. I also believe that a patient's faith is supported and enhanced by the physician's faith and additionally strengthened and supported by the prayers of the church. This patient's situation seemed almost hopeless, but she had a strong faith in God. We both prayed mightily, as did others for her.

She proceeded with the standard treatment for her condition, which included surgery, radiation therapy, and chemotherapy. After the treatment, her cancer completely disappeared. There was no further evidence of disease. It has been ten years since her treatment, and still there is no evidence of disease.

Against all odds, and against our scientific understanding, she was healed. The outcome surprised everyone because it was not logical. It did not surprise me because I believe that faith can heal us. Clearly the God who created us, the heavens, and the earth can certainly reverse the course of an illness. Jesus said, "What is impossible with men is possible with God" (Luke 18:27).

Who decides who lives and who dies? Those who are supposed to die sometimes live, while those who are supposed to live sometimes die. The ultimate decision obviously is not ours but comes from the Father. Therefore, it is to the Father that we must address our petitions.

"Your faith has healed you" (Luke 18:42). This phrase is repeated many times in the gospel, stressing the importance of faith in our own healing. It explains why some physicians, including myself, practice holistic medicine. By holistic medicine I mean we strive to address and heal the whole person, mind and spirit, not just the body. I must testify that I have personally encountered many instances in which the standard treatment fails to heal a person, but the person is healed when a spiritual sickness is addressed.

Spiritual Sickness

Just as there is physical sickness, there is also spiritual sickness. Unconfessed sin causes spiritual sickness. It separates us from God and leads to the destruction of the soul. It is the Spirit that lights up our soul. Without its healing power, we are plunged into darkness.

I remember a patient who often came to my office with multiple complaints and great underlying anxiety. She would never completely improve from the original problem before yet another health problem would beset her. But one day, tired of not getting anywhere with her healing, she finally broke down and opened up to me. She explained how she had been wounded in the past by the person she trusted most in her life, her husband. She had anger and unforgiveness in her heart for what he had done to her. She thought about his offense every day, and consciously or unconsciously, negative feelings dominated her life. Her spirit within was sick.

It was not until she gave up her anger and chose forgivingness that she was able to improve in her physical health. She was filled with peace. Every visit thereafter, her peace was evident and transformational. She became a different person. Even though she developed cancer years later, she was able to overcome it and is now a long-term survivor.

We can choose to be healed from our spiritual sickness as well as from our physical sickness. We can be completely healed by the power of the name of Jesus, which is not to be recited as a magical incantation, but by the power of faith.

True and total healing is from God. Healing of the complete person involves healing from physical infirmities as well as from the torment of evil spirits (see Acts 5:16). True and complete healing is healing of the body, mind, and spirit.

Choose a Good Death: Accepting God's Will

Sometimes healing fails to be achieved despite the best science, technology, and faith. We experience progressive illness. Despite our fervent prayers, God chooses not to heal us in the ways we think He should. It is then that we must trust even more in Him and accept His wisdom. We must recognize that nobody is meant to live forever, and that our time here on earth is also limited.

Man's entire life is in a way a preparation for the last, ultimate moment of life, the moment of death, when man becomes one with God and enters immortality or eternity. Man returns to the source of which he was made: his body to the earth, for "dust you are and to dust you will return" (Genesis 3:19); his soul unto the fullness of God. For the believer, death does not mean destruction, but a step into a greater life with God, being found in Him. "For as in Adam all die, so in Christ all will be made alive" (1 Corinthians 15:22).

The experience of death can occur in many different ways: it can be consciously or unconsciously; it can also be an act of giving up life into the hands of God as a last, sacrificial event (which can be called a good death or dying right); or it can be an act of having life taken away with struggle and without peace (which can be called a bad death). This struggle comes from unbelief and from lack of faith; it is the result of not trusting in God's promises. It represents a last attempt to hold on to what we cannot hold on to because it is not ours.

Persons who are selfish and self-centered, whose life pursuits were focused upon the acquisition of things, will have trouble giving up, at the moment of death, all those things they acquired in life. They will struggle in a last, futile attempt to hang on to them, refusing to give them up. For them, their death will be more like the taking of a life and an act of violence rather than a peaceful giving. In a sense, those who die this way die as they have lived.

The choice of good death is the last conscious act in life before eternity. Eternity means a "forever now," always in the present; it means the end of time—no more past and no more future.

For us believers and followers of Christ, the end of our earthly life is also the beginning of the best part of our journey, eternal life. A seed must die in order for new life to emerge. As He was about to face His own death, Jesus said, "I tell you the truth, unless a kernel of wheat falls to the ground and dies, it remains only a single seed. But if it dies, it produces many seeds" (John 12:24).

No matter what the outcome, whether we are healed or continue to experience progressive sickness and deterioration, may we receive the fullness of God's love as a result of choosing His true and total healing. It is my sincere hope that as we look at the twilight of our life, we can sense the abundant harvest that is to come from the seeds we planted during our lives. May our life produce an abundant harvest of souls, and may our dying seed become a large tree in the garden of God.

CHAPTER 15

CHOOSE WISDOM OVER FOOLISHNESS

They call him "Dokta Jim." Wherever he goes, he is instantly recognized and treated with great respect. Everybody knows his four-wheel drive, white SUV with the logo "Church of the Nazarene" painted on its doors as he travels down the winding and sometimes dangerous roads of the countryside. For more than twenty years, he has been one of Kudjip's miracle worker physicians who, with very limited resources, has been able to produce astounding results in this remote village of Papua New Guinea.

Dokta Jim has been there when children in the village develop "pot belly" intestinal obstruction from eating "beetle juice" seeds. He has mended their broken bodies after "chop-chop" machete injuries that result from tribal warfare or domestic violence. He has been the doctor of last resort when women nearly hemorrhage to death after giving birth.

Being the only surgeon for a population of 250,000, he works endless hours: day and night, week after week, year after year. On Sundays he preaches the gospel at bush churches. He is a full-time medical missionary of the Church of the Nazarene to Papua New Guinea. His name is Jim Radcliffe.

Jim's wife, Kathy, shares his vision and his dream. Jim and Kathy have six children, the majority born in Papua New Guinea. Looking after them, preparing the meals, and supporting their programs and activities is a full-time job that Kathy manages with great devotion and grace. She also teaches classes for missionary children and participates in women's ministries and in other church programs.

My wife and I consider it a great blessing to know Jim and Kathy and to have shared with them in the work of the church in Papua New Guinea and at the mission hospital.

One may ask what led them to their unique calling in this faraway place, and what they have that makes their lives full and complete. As I look into their lives, I find the answers. With great reverence for God, they sought His counsel and advice when they were young people. They dedicated themselves to God and devoted their lives to the service of others. They had a vision for their lives that put God first and that was uplifting of others. They also nurtured the essential relationships in life, succeeding in their family life as well as in their work. Their lives display the choice of wisdom.

Obtaining Wisdom

Wisdom is something to be sought and pursued. It is a hidden treasure uncovered through diligent search. Effort is required to find it—it is not a given in anyone's life. Wisdom is acquired through thoughtful analysis and the counsel and advice of other wise people before action is taken. Wisdom is not instinctive or impulsive; it is measured and calculated.

Where do we find wisdom? Wisdom begins and ends with God. Psalm 111:10 says it clearly: "The fear of the Lord is the beginning of wisdom; all who follow his precepts have good understanding." Fear of the Lord is reverence for God. Knowing God and following His commands are the foundation of all wisdom. Wisdom is not gained by experience and academic pursuits alone, but from the knowledge of God.

Wisdom is not measured in facts, social status, or even in educational level. It is not directly correlated to IQ. Instead, it is a basic approach to knowledge about relationships and the world that leads to measured, analytical, and carefully thought-out responses to life's basic problems. Wisdom includes making good use of knowledge.

Wisdom and knowledge are not the same. Knowledge is a collection of raw facts and data without analysis. Wisdom is careful analysis of data and a response that is commensurate and appropriate to the data. Knowledge is easily available and easily accessed. Wisdom is scarce and hard to come by.

Characteristics of the Wise

These are some salient characteristics of those who have wisdom:

1. <u>Vision</u>. The wise have a vision of what they want to do, where they want to go, and how they can get there. People with vision have a plan and a destination; they set goals and move steadily toward fulfilling them. The clearer and more detailed their vision and the more realistic it is, the more attainable it will become.
2. <u>Thought before action</u>. The wise think before speaking and before taking action. They measure the consequences of their words and of their actions.
3. <u>Uplifting others</u>. The wise uplift others, not tear them down. Their wise actions and projects benefit others, improving them and the circumstances in their lives.
4. <u>Search for God's counsel and advice</u>. No project or plan is ever undertaken by the wise without prayer and petition, submitting all thoughts and requests to God.
5. <u>Search for expert opinion</u>. The wise seek the counsel of experts or other wise people who have experience in a particular matter or have special knowledge or insight. The wise admit that they do not have all the answers, and they are not too proud to ask for others' opinions and input. The wise surround themselves with other wise people that will support them in their quest and help them succeed.
6. <u>Diligence</u>. The wise are characterized by diligence. They work extra hard, often putting more effort than what seems

necessary to assure the success of a project. Not surprisingly, they achieve success more often than those who just invest the bare minimum effort.

7. <u>Discipline and organization</u>. The wise are disciplined and organized. They think out all possible scenarios and are ready for all eventualities. All is well planned. Discipline is defined by *Webster's Dictionary* (11th ed.) as the training of the mind and character. It is to put all areas of life under control.

It is essential that we who are followers of Christ seek and pursue wisdom for our lives. We need the wisdom that comes from God about all areas of life, including work and family, children, finances, our communities, and the world.

King Solomon's ultimate conclusion in the book of Ecclesiastes is that the wisdom of the wise is meaningless without God. When we place in His hands what little or much wisdom we have, we reach our ultimate goal and true potential.

More Characteristics of the Wise

The wise are known for excellence in their work. They have a clear understanding of the significance and purpose of their work, and they are cognizant of the effort needed to succeed. They devote every effort and time necessary for success. They do not accept mediocrity.

The wise are careful stewards of their money. They measure expenses and are not impulsive spenders, gamblers, or squanderers. They depend on their efforts to achieve their wealth, not on chance or the lotto.

The wise do not succeed at work while failing in all other important aspects of life. Instead, they intentionally devote the time and effort necessary to nurture and prosper the essential relationships of life—relationships with family and children. Their wise actions include strong spiritual leadership of their families. They demonstrate with the example of their life the importance of Christian values. With love, encouragement, and discipline, they pass on to their children their passion for excellence.

The wise recognize their responsibility as bearers of the light and the importance of passing their light to the next generation. Their life narrative displays a "theme song" with vision, mission, and purpose; the many windows that look into their soul radiate a bright light.

Wisdom about the World

Wisdom about our lives implies wisdom about our communities and wisdom about the world. Wise people understand that they do not live isolated in a time capsule, but that they live in a world where what happens to others affects them and vice versa. The wise, therefore, seek the well-being and prosperity of all humanity.

As English poet and clergyman John Donne (1572–1631) eloquently wrote in his essay "Meditation XVII": "No man is an island, entire of itself; every man is a piece of the continent, a part of the main ... any man's death diminishes me, because I am involved in mankind." Wise people also recognize their connection with humanity; they are "involved in mankind."

The Foolish

The foolish, also called sluggards in the Bible, are characterized by laziness, hastiness, impulsiveness, ignorance, arrogance, irresponsibility, and self-centeredness. Sluggards lack vision, focus, and, most importantly, the power of God and His wisdom in their lives. "The fear of the Lord is the beginning of knowledge, but fools despise wisdom and discipline" (Proverbs 1:7).

Contrary to the wise, the foolish are undisciplined and unorganized. They fail to play by the rules and are in frequent conflict with their spouses, their bosses, and the authorities. Fools lack self-control, and as a result give full vent to their anger (see Proverbs 29:11); their mouth is their undoing (see Proverbs 18:7). Thus they are frequently involved in arguments and heated discussions. They do not seek or accept counsel or advice; they like to go at it alone because they think they know better. Because they fail to consider all possible scenarios, they also fail more often in their jobs and family life.

Fools often miss educational, professional development or career opportunities because these require hard work, self-discipline, and self-sacrifice. They'd rather take the easy way out and are, consequently, average or mediocre workers. They also seek easy fortune and are often compulsive spenders and gamblers.

This portrait of the foolish applies to those who, despite their God-given gifts and abilities, fail to put what they have available to good use in meeting the challenges and opportunities that life brings. Excluded are people with mental or learning disabilities who fail to reach their true potential because of these disabilities.

Because the foolish lack God's presence and wisdom, their life narrative lacks a "theme song." They lack vision, mission, and purpose for life. The windows that look into their soul are small and opaque and project a dim light.

Wisdom Leads to Abundant Life

In order to have an abundant life here on earth, it is essential that we seek wisdom and pursue it. We must focus on the truly important things in life. Chief among them are the knowledge of God and obedience to His commandments. We must also make good use of the knowledge we acquire and apply it to all aspects of our life, including our work, family, and relationships. Wisdom requires that we are good stewards of all that has been given to us.

"A man who loves wisdom brings joy to his father" (Proverbs 29:3). May our lives be filled with wisdom and bring joy to our heavenly Father.

CHAPTER 16
CHOOSE FORGIVENESS OVER UNFORGIVINGNESS

The fall of the South Africa regime of apartheid in 1994 symbolized the triumph of freedom over oppression, of right over wrong, of justice over injustice. The policies of the regime had taken away the human rights and the civil rights of the 90 percent black majority of the country, while granting the 10 percent white minority all the privileges and rights. Under apartheid, blacks were uprooted from their ancestral homelands and made to live in townships with substandard housing, health services, public services, and education. They could not travel freely in their own country except with a permit, and they were forced to learn Afrikaans, the language of the white minority. They were educated only enough to be of use to the apartheid regime.

After many years of struggle, this oppressive system was finally dismantled. In the April 1994 election, the African National Congress (ANC) party was allowed to participate and had an overwhelming electoral victory. This victory ushered Nelson Mandela into the presidency of South Africa, making him the nation's first elected black president.

It was widely feared that the new government would unleash a retaliatory campaign of pillage, violence, and murder against the white minority in retribution for the crimes of apartheid. Instead, the improbable happened. Nelson Mandela set the agenda for a peaceful transfer of power. With great wisdom and love for his country, he embraced forgiveness. That forgiveness was linked to disclosure of grievances and restitution of what had been taken away.

South Africa's success story is about forgiveness: a country's forgiveness. Forgiveness allowed the country to move forward, leaving behind the injustices of apartheid, and to focus on the building of a new South Africa, where people of all skin colors could live together in peace, with equal rights and opportunities.

A New Start through Forgiveness

Forgiveness is a basic pillar of our Christian faith. Scripture states that God forgives us of all our sins, no matter how serious. The Lord "forgives all your sins" (Psalm 103:3). Yes, God is willing to forgive all sins as long as we sincerely repent. His capacity to forgive fills us with awe as we consider it. Like the prophet, we can exclaim, "Who is a God like you, who pardons sin and forgives the transgression" (Micah 7:18).

As God forgives our sins, so must we also forgive those who sin against us. "Forgive, and you will be forgiven" (Luke 6:37).

Forgiveness gives us the capacity to make a new start, allowing us to rise up from the mire of sin and to have another chance. Likewise, when we forgive others, we restore their ability to have a new beginning while maintaining their dignity; we restore them in relationship to us without humbling or debasing them.

A Wife's Forgiveness

A woman in her mid-forties lay on a bed in the surgical ward at the Kudjip Nazarene Hospital in Papua New Guinea, recovering from recent surgery. She had a long line of neatly placed surgical staples going across her face, starting in the left check, continuing over the bridge of the nose, and onto the right cheek. One side of her face was drooping due to nerve injury, and blood-tinged saliva drooled from her partially opened mouth. Her face appeared grotesquely distorted due to the severity of the swelling.

The violent slashes of a machete had left defensive wounds in both her arms, and three fingers were missing from her right hand. The violence against her also had left her with deep psychological wounds. From her swollen shut eyes, tears rolled down her cheeks. She was stunned, perplexed, and deeply hurt. Her husband had done this to her.

During her long hospital stay, she received pastoral care that helped her deal with her psychological wounds. They were more difficult to heal than her physical ones. After several weeks, she accepted her husband's earnest apologies and forgave him. By that time, she was strong enough to return home.

In Papua New Guinea, patients must be able to walk home upon discharge from the hospital because, more often than not, they must walk back to their villages. Western physicians practicing in Papua New Guinea must quickly adjust to this reality; they must set aside the Western impulse toward short hospital stays.

This woman, disfigured and disabled by her husband, made the choice to forgive him and to walk back and take her place once again as his wife.

The Transforming Power of the Gospel

In Papua, as in many parts of the world, domestic violence is prevalent, and women are frequently the victims. Societal views of women as property of their husbands are largely responsible for their victimization. This devaluing of women stems from the tradition of "wife buying," in which a man must pay a price to the family of his intended bride before he is allowed to marry her. The price is set according to the prospective bride's attributes and years of education. Payments are usually made partially in Kina (the local currency) and partially in livestock (a herd of pigs).

Polygamy is also at the root of domestic violence because it breeds discontent and animosity among members of a family. The inability to bear children (infertility) is considered a curse, and it too is a contributing factor.

Christianity has had a dramatic impact upon these practices and upon societal views of women. Believers learn about the sanctity of marriage, as being the union of one man and only one woman: "For this reason a man will leave his father and mother and be united to his wife, and the two will become one flesh" (Matthew 19:5). They learn the Christian view of women as partners to their husbands and the admonition to husbands to submit to their wives: "Husbands, love your wives, just as Christ loved the church" (Ephesians 5:25). The uplifting of women that occurs as a result is a testimony of the power of the gospel to transform lives and to transform society.

Unforgiveness Hurts Us

Some people are unwilling to forgive others for their offenses. They hold their offenders accountable and keep a grudge against them indefinitely. Their relationships are permanently damaged by the offenses. Others are willing to forgive only minor offenses but draw the line for major offenses, which are deemed unforgivable. Still others feel like they need to take their time to grant forgiveness. The longer they take to forgive, the more difficult forgiveness becomes. They give Satan room to work by allowing bitterness to settle into their souls.

Unforgiveness actually hurts us more than it hurts others. It makes us angry and resentful. "In your anger do not sin. Do not let the sun go down while you are still angry" (Ephesians 4:26).

If we ignore this admonition, it causes a root of bitterness to grow in us. It slowly corrodes and destroys the soul.

What Happens When We Forgive

Forgiveness is a process; it is a chain of events that leads to abundant life. The first step in the process is choosing to forgive.

"What about my rights?" some may say, reflecting the legalistic society in which we live. The simple answer is that when we choose to forgive, we give up our rights. By forgiving we are actually saying, "Even though you hurt me, I release you, and I give up the right to hurt you back." In so doing, we release ourselves from the burden of unforgiveness. And as we set others free, we also free ourselves.

Forgiveness is hard, and it comes with a cost. We give up some of our ego and permanently give up our rights. But our cost pales in comparison to the cost paid for our forgiveness, the life of God's one and only Son.

When we forgive, we must also be willing to forget. We cannot forgive and keep revisiting in our mind what offended us. We must be willing to part with its memory, destroying permanently all mental record of the offense. We must forget the offense as God forgets our offenses. It is as King David describes: "As far as the east is from the west, so far has he removed our transgressions from us" (Psalm 103:12).

More than anything we can say with words, forgiveness speaks volumes about our faith. It is putting our faith into action. It is tangible proof that we possess salvation. And it is a powerful testimony to others who are watching how we choose to live.

Forgiving Ourselves

One more aspect of forgiveness requires our attention. It, too, is part of living the abundant life.

Many times in our Christian walk we carry the burdens of our forgiven sins because we cannot forgive ourselves. These sins have been forgiven because we have confessed them to God and those we offended, but we mistakenly continue to hold ourselves accountable for them. Not only must we forgive others, but we must forgive ourselves.

To be forgiven is to have our debt cancelled, which is equivalent to being set free. Having been set free, we must then give up our feelings of guilt so that we can receive God's grace and comfort. "So if the Son sets you free, you will be free indeed" (John 8:36). This final step in the process of the forgiveness of our own sins is essential in order to enjoy the abundant life that God has promised to all who love Him.

The Price of Our Forgiveness

As I reflected upon an example to illustrate this chapter on forgiveness, I was drawn time and time again to the crucifixion of Jesus Christ that Friday afternoon about 2,000 years ago at Golgotha.

Jesus was betrayed by one of his friends, who handed Him over to the religious leaders. He was arrested and brought in front of the governor out of the envy of religious leaders. The uproar of the crowd promoted the governor to declare Him guilty, although He had no fault. He was flogged, beaten, mocked, and humiliated. His other friends denied knowing Him and scattered in fear. He was sentenced to die a most cruel death: the slow, painful, and agonizing death of crucifixion.

He carried His cross through the city and up to Golgotha, where He was crucified between two thieves. Nails were driven through his hands and feet, and He was pierced in the flank with a spear. As He was dying, He gave the world the greatest and best example of forgiveness. He forgave those who were crucifying him: "Father, forgive them, for they do not know what they are doing" (Luke 23:34). He then gave up His spirit.

There was no reason or justification for His execution. It was unjust, unfair, and undeserved.

For a moment it seemed that the forces of evil had scored a victory. Evil and death seemed to have had the upper hand. Three days later, God raised Him from the dead. His resurrection proved that He had triumphed over death; it also proved that death had no hold on Him, and that evil had been defeated. His death was the price paid for our forgiveness.

Humanity's ultimate destiny rests upon its acceptance of the message that was proclaimed at Golgotha 2,000 years ago. Implicit in our forgiveness is that we also extend our forgiveness to others.

Forgiveness opens the door to the abundant life that God has planned for us. We must choose to walk through this door.

CHAPTER 17

CHOOSE HONESTY OVER DISHONESTY

No person alive can ever claim perfection or to be above errors of commission or omission. Nobody can claim sanctity and deny being a sinner. To do so would be dishonest.

Like you, I have not always made the right choices in life or taken the right stand on every issue. I have made mistakes in my life, and I recognize that I am a sinner. But I also know that I am saved by faith in God and His grace, and that I am forgiven. God chose me, as he chose you, to do good works. I want my honest, personal confession to frame this important chapter on honesty.

Similarly, we must all be honest with each other. James 5:16 says, "Confess your sins to each other and pray for each other so that you may be healed."

The Display of Honesty

Honesty is defined as the display of truthfulness and integrity; being upright, in a right relationship with God.

Second Kings 12 describes the story of Joash, King of Judah, who in his younger years "did what was right in the eyes of the Lord" (2 Kings 12:2). He instructed the priests in the temple to collect all the money that was given as sacred offerings for use in the repair of the temple. After twenty-three years, the priests had not obeyed his instruction. He then appointed his royal secretary and the high priest to take charge, counting the money and paying the workers. An accounting was not required "because they acted with complete honesty" (2 Kings 12:15).

This example shows how honest people can be trusted to do God's work. Honesty is a characteristic of the righteous; they steadfastly uphold the truth. They are pure and honest, bathed in the light. Regrettably, some allow darkness and untruth to enter their lives. Dishonesty transforms them.

The Mask of Dishonesty

In his later years, King Joash chose the ways of dishonesty. He listened to those who wore the mask of dishonesty, allowed the progressive erosion of his righteousness, and was transformed into a cruel, dishonest person. He departed from the Lord so far that he ordered the stoning to death of the prophet Zechariah (see 2 Chronicles 24:17–26). The Lord then removed His favor from King Joash, permitting his kingdom to be conquered by Arameans. King Joash then died an ignominious death at the hand of assassins. Dishonesty has consequences.

If we, like Joash, allow ourselves to succumb to the secular culture of our times, listening to its advisors, it would seem permissible to alter the truth in order to fit our needs. We must resist the corruptive influence of our culture and steadfastly cling to the truth. We must display honesty and integrity always and without exceptions.

Despite our best intention, there will be times when we digress and deviate from the truth. At such times, we must recognize our failures and confess our sins. We must then resume our journey in honesty and integrity. If Joash had done so, his story would certainly have had a different ending.

A Portrait of Honesty

Dr. Susan Myers is a medical missionary of the Church of the Nazarene to Papua New Guinea. A pastor's daughter, she grew up in the church. At an early age, she dedicated her life to the Lord and wanted to be a missionary. After her graduation from medical school and residency program, she became a medical missionary.

As a pediatrician, Dr. Meyers works long hours in the pediatric ward at the Kudjip Nazarene Hospital. Among her many responsibilities is the treatment of women with an abnormal Papanicolaou smear (a screening test for cervical cancer). Her ministry to women and children has made her an iconic figure in the eyes of women in Papua New Guinea.

In a society where women are subservient to men and hold a lower standing, Dr. Meyers is also an example and an inspiration to women. Her life shows that it is perfectly possible to be an outstanding medical professional and, at the same time, to be a dedicated mother and wife.

This woman's life displays honesty. With truthfulness and integrity, in a right relationship with God, she serves God by caring for women and children in Papua New Guinea.

Admitting Our Responsibility

From the example of the life of King Joash of Judah, we can discern that failure to be honest with one another is a root cause of problems in relationships, business, politics, and world affairs. Our failure to make this most basic choice has consequences for us and for the whole world.

If we are honest with each other about the state of our world today, we must admit our faults and responsibility: for the great acts of injustice, for the growing disparity between the rich and the poor, for the death of millions of human beings from preventable causes, for not addressing the crippling poverty of the great majority of our brothers and sisters.

No doubt we are living in times of great humanitarian crisis and great spiritual darkness, but where are the world's two billion Christians in the face of these problems? Regrettably, most of the time we have been missing in action.

Previous chapters have looked at how choices have impacted segregation and the civil rights movement of the 1960s, apartheid in South Africa, Nazism, and discrimination against minorities. Except for a few isolated voices, the church was silent during these times of extreme evil and injustice.

As members of the church, are we choosing to blame the darkness instead of acting as the light to the world? Are we blaming others for the spiritual staleness of the world instead of being the salt of the earth? Are we comfortable within the four walls of our church while failing to address the glaring needs of others outside those walls?

We, mere humans, are the church of Jesus Christ, who is the Savior of the world. Each one of us represents Him. We are His ambassadors—and we have failed. "We are therefore Christ's ambassadors, as though God were making his appeal through us" (2 Corinthians 5:20). We have not stood up for the truth. We have been quick to assign responsibility to others; we have been dishonest.

If there is moral decay in our world, it is because we have not been diligent enough in being the light of the world and the salt of the earth. If there is hunger in the world, it is because we have failed at the fair and just distribution of what is produced. If there is disease and war, it is because we have lacked the will and moral courage to put an end to them.

Let us be honest with ourselves and ask why there has been so little progress in solving the enormous problems that affect the world. Let's face it. Many of these problems persist because we have lacked the will to solve them, even though we have had the ability.

Honesty and the Problem of Hunger

The Food and Agriculture organization (FAO) of the United Nations estimates that one of every six citizens of the world is malnourished

(1.02 billion people). Despite progress in economic development in some areas of the world, many of the world's peoples are still being left behind. The percentage of hungry people in the world in 2010 is higher than in 1970, the first year that statistics were made available. The year 2009 was particularly devastating for the world's hungry, largely due to the world economic crisis (www.fao.org/hunger statistics).

The most recent FAO statistics show that most of the world's hungry people live in Asia and the Pacific (642 million) and in sub-Sahara Africa (265 million). There is hunger in the Caribbean (53 million people) and even in developed countries (15 million).

Also according to FAO, at the beginning of the twenty-first century, world hunger was for the most part caused by crop failures and drought. More recently, it has been on the increase in our nation due to high domestic food prices, lower incomes, and unemployment.

Sources that monitor agriculture (www.fao.org) know that the world now produces enough food to meet the minimum caloric requirement of all of its people (2,350 calories per day for every adult). For the first time in history, we have the resources to eradicate hunger. The issue now is whether we have the will (www.fao.org)

Changing the World by Our Works

The gospel is not only about winning souls but also about transforming society and changing the world by our works. Honesty is about standing for the truth and about being sincere. Let us look at ourselves in the mirror and ask, "Where is our fruit, and which are our works?"

I am absolutely convinced that the world would be a different place if the two billion Christians living right now were honest in accepting the admonitions contained in the gospel to have works that glorify God. We all have received different talents, and God expects us to use those talents to further His kingdom here on earth. One of my favorite Scripture passages is the parable of the loaned money, or the talents.

The kingdom of heaven is "like a man going on a journey, who called his servants and entrusted his property to them. To one he gave five talents of money, to another two talents, and to another one talent, each according to his ability" (Matthew 25:14–15).

Similarly, God has given us different amounts of money according to our ability, and He expects a return on what He entrusted to us. Even our abilities are not ours, but God's gift, to be used for His purpose. "Whoever can be trusted with very little can also be trusted with much, and whoever is dishonest with very little will also be dishonest with much (Luke 16:10). Our call.

We are honest when we stand for the truth, not only with our words but also with actions, not only with our faith but also with our works.

CHAPTER 18
CHOOSE MAKING A DIFFERENCE OVER BEING INDIFFERENT

Nobel Peace Laureate and former United States president Jimmy Carter declared in his Nobel lecture given in Oslo, Norway, on December 10, 2002, that the number one problem facing the world today is the growing disparity between the rich and the poor. Richard Sterns, CEO of World Vision, in his book, *The Hole in the Gospel* (Thomas Nelson, 2009), explains that the average person living in the third world today has seventy-five times less income than the average person living in the first world (USA, Canada, Western Europe, and Australia). Famine and poverty are entrenched, chronic problems in the great majority of the world, while the upper one third of the world's population consumes the majority of the world's goods and services.

The statistics are dumfounding and staggering. Sterns' book details them. For example, of the 6.7 billion population of the world today, one billion people live in extreme poverty, defined by the United Nations as living on less than one dollar per day. Compare that to the average U.S. salary of $38,000 per year, which is over $100 per day. Only 0.3 billion people (4.5 percent of the world's population) command this income (122).

Poverty is not only a matter of low income but also a lack of public health, clean water, and sanitation. Often these circumstances are linked to poor governance, greed, corruption, and system failures. Such system failures also cause the oppression and disenfranchisement of women in some cultures that bar them from property ownership or education. Poverty, too, is the result of wars and violence that cause forced migrations of people running away from the conflict, creating humanitarian crises of large proportions. Natural disasters such as tsunamis and drought with crop failures are contributing factors of poverty as well.

So the majority of the world is poor, and the majority in our nation is rich. It follows, then, that the rich should have responsibility for the poor; that those who have plenty should share with those who lack. We can choose to make a difference.

The Biblical Law of Sharing

The Old Testament law mandated the sharing of resources as a matter of routine for those who owned fields and vineyards. Scripture says, "When you reap the harvest of your land, do not reap to the very edges of your field or gather the gleanings of your harvest. Do not go over your vineyard a second time or pick up the grapes that have fallen. Leave them for the poor and the alien" (Leviticus 19: 9–10).

It is thought by many that if those who have so much could share with those who do not, most of the world's problems would cease to exist. Perhaps this is a simplistic approach because the problem of poverty is rather complex, but if each of us shared with at least one other person who has less, it would go a long way toward solving the problem.

Indifference for the Suffering of Others

Aggravating and exacerbating all the contributing factors to poverty are the unresponsiveness and the indifference of the well-to-do. It is unconscionable that, for example, ten million children die every year from preventable causes such as malaria, TB, HIV/AIDS, and hunger related conditions (www.worldvision.org/poverty), and yet their plight only rarely catches our attention. These problems are so widespread that they cease to be news; most of the time they do not even garner a headline in our daily papers or a sound bite in our newscasts. Just consider the magnitude of the problem: 26,000 children die every day from preventable causes, and the world does not take notice (www.worldvision.org/poverty).

In my mind one of the greatest sins is the sin of indifference toward the suffering of others. It is to be comfortable in our abundance and not to see the needs of others. The poor then become invisible. The death of their children becomes a statistic that does not affect us, being rationalized as the inevitable outcome of things beyond our control. This is wrong, outrageously wrong!

In the book of Amos (6:1–6), the Scripture says, "Woe to you who are complacent in Zion, and to you who feel secure … you do not grieve over the ruin of Joseph." It means that those who are complacent and comfortable with their life and do not grieve over the suffering of the world do not receive God's favor but deserve God's wrath.

My Awakening

I once was comfortable in my own safety and abundance, and I thought, as many do, that system failures were the cause of poverty, and poverty was something beyond my control. One day my wife and I attended a missions conference in Louisville, Kentucky, where Richard Sterns was a keynote speaker. He spoke about the comfort and indifference of many in the church in the face of the greatest humanitarian crisis the world had ever seen: the HIV/AIDS epidemic in Africa. He compared the yearly death toll of the HIV/AIDS epidemic of 3,000,000 people to three 9/11s every day or to a Holocaust every two years. He declared that the church has become complacent and has not responded appropriately to this epidemic. He urged all those there to become involved.

As my wife and I pondered his talk and our response to it, we asked God to show us how to become involved. First we thought we would sponsor an orphan of the HIV/AIDS epidemic through World Vision. But God said, "Good, but not enough. I want you to sponsor a village."

A village? How could two ordinary people do this?

God said, "I will show you the way."

We then asked God to show us a place. The country of Swaziland in Africa stood prominently in our minds, because it had the highest HIV infection rate in the world (on the order of 33 percent), which meant that one of every three Swazi citizens was HIV positive (www.who.org/HIV statistics). We chose Swaziland also because our church, the Church of the Nazarene, has a large presence in that country. It operates the largest hospital, the Raleigh Fitkin Memorial Hospital, and there are numerous Nazarene clinics, schools, and seminaries in that country.

Our next step was to ask World Vision to give us a village in Swaziland. We received N'cina, part of the Mpolongeni Community Development Project. My wife and I then went to numerous Nazarene churches in our church district and spoke about the HIV/AIDS epidemic in Africa and the need for the church to become involved. We succeeded in obtaining the sponsorship of approximately a hundred orphans and vulnerable children, and God also gave us the ability to help finance the Mpolongeni project.

This Area Development Project (ADP) includes eleven villages that are now receiving clean water from water wells, latrines, microfinancing, animal husbandry assistance with goat farms to provide food and family income, and seed for drought-resistant crops that can thrive in this country, which has just experienced seven years of drought. This ADP also provides community organization and empowerment to care for those ill with AIDS and to locate and look after the orphans. It emphasizes a culture of community self-sufficiency and empowerment rather than a culture of dependency.

In 2008, my wife and daughter and I went to Swaziland with World Vision to visit our five sponsored children. We went to meet them, state our support, and offer the love and comfort of God. We also visited our ADP and the different projects in those villages. It was an extraordinary experience to see God's work through our small efforts to make a difference; how God transformed our desire to help one child into something bigger and better that now encompasses eleven villages. We saw how God is restoring hope in those communities, which are the poorest of the poor, and how the next generation of Swazi children now has a chance of survival.

This testimony is given not for our own credit but for God's credit, as our credit is not from man but from God. It is given in the interest of the people of the third world who are waiting for the people of the first world to act. It is an example of how God can use ordinary people to do great things.

A Different Perspective on Poverty

From a public health perspective, much more can be accomplished. It is better to teach people how to stay healthy and how to prevent disease than to care for them in clinics or refugee camps after they are ill. It is far more effective and impacting to help them drill clean water wells and latrines than to treat cholera and other causes of diarrhea. It is better to develop drought-resistant crops and make them widely available than to have to treat malnutrition. It is wiser to invest in microfinancing schemes than to invest large sums of money in salvage and relief operations.

I do not mean to imply that other humanitarian strategies are useless. On the contrary, all are important in addressing immediate needs that need urgent solutions. But from a public health perspective, it is better to give the poor a "hand up" instead of a "hand down." A hand up seeks long-term solutions by fostering self-reliance and self-sufficiency. A hand down encourages dependency and can potentially transform people into beggars that continually ask for more.

The old adage still rings true: "If you give a man a fish, he will eat once; but if you teach him how to fish, he will eat every day." Simply stated, giving someone in need a meal is not bad in and of itself, because it is our responsibility before God to do so; it is better, however, to teach him to feed himself so that he can eat every day.

Relief and Development

Relief and development are two different approaches to the problems of poverty. Each one has its place, and each one addresses a particular need.

Relief provides a short-term solution to an immediate need, such as food, clothing, or shelter. Though often essential in times of crisis, it can have unintended, negative consequences over the long term, such as stifling local entrepreneurs and destroying a fragile local economy. For instance, a well-intended clothing donation to a village allows villagers to be clothed for a while; but if clothes are provided regularly, local clothing stores will close for lack of business, and local clothing manufactures will have no one to buy their goods. Therefore, it is imperative that relief operations are carefully thought out and all possible consequences measured. Since there is no replacement for personal involvement, relief efforts that operate through person-to-person connections have the maximum desired effect.

Development, in contrast, is a long-term investment in the future of others and a long-term commitment to their success. It seeks to empower individuals to find solutions to their own problems. There is widespread consensus that charity without appropriate understanding and engagement with the poor risks failure. It is important, therefore, to seek long-term strategies that are effective and successful. Microfinancing is one such strategy. Through it, small loans of money are made to individuals in order to finance cottage industries and businesses. These small businesses provide new sources of income to individuals and new resources for communities. These small sums are administered by a group of people from the community who expect the debts to be repaid so that others can benefit as well.

Choosing to Make a Difference

In the eyes of God, it does not matter what approach we take, whether it is a hand up or a hand down, a relief or a development operation. The most important thing is to decide to take our personal responsibility to heart and to take action.

The antidote for complacency and indifference starts with the decision to make a difference; it starts with the determination to become involved in solving the number one problem of the world, which is the increasing gap between the rich and the poor.

I believe it is important to see poverty and the suffering of the world firsthand and grieve over it. It will change your life, as it changed mine. When you see it, grieve over it, and ask God what you can do, you will no longer be comfortable in your abundance.

God's Judgment for Indifference

The book of Revelation contains the apostle John's vision of God's judgment for the church. One of the harshest judgments is reserved for the church of Sardis: "I have not found your deeds complete in the sight of my God" (Revelation 3:2). Severe judgment is also passed on the church in Laodicea: "I know your deeds, that you are neither cold nor hot ... So, because you are lukewarm—neither hot nor cold—I am about to spit you out of my mouth" (Revelation 3:15–16). There is judgment also for the church in Ephesus: "Yet I hold this against you: You have forsaken your first love (Revelation 2:4).

What would be God's judgment for the church in the United States of America? Would God find our deeds to be complete in His sight? Would God find us to be lukewarm, or to be passionate, decisive, and committed to Him and to the service of others? Would He find that we have always remembered our first love, which is our love for Him, to be what motivates our thoughts and our deeds?

God knows every church and every one of us. It is my sincere hope that when God renders His judgment on us, He finds us to have been ardent, faithful, and obedient in making a difference in the world, as He leads us. May He find that our deeds are complete in His sight, and that we have always remembered our first love.

CHAPTER 19
CHOOSE JUSTICE OVER INJUSTICE

The question of what God expects of us after our lives have been enlightened by the gospel is all-important, because on it hinges how we will be judged when this life is over. As in the parable in Matthew 25:14–30, each of us will answer to what we did with the "talents" we received: whether we put them to good use for the service of others or wasted them on selfish pursuits. And as in the metaphor Jesus used for what we are to do with the gospel in Luke 11:33, we will be asked if we hid the "lamp" of God's grace under a table or if we placed it on a stand so that it could shine into the lives of those living in the darkness.

Will we be counted among those who actively pursue justice?

The Two Cities

In his book, *The City of God*, early Christian theologian Augustine states that there are two kinds of love that determine the human response to suffering and justice. He illustrates them by dividing human beings into two different camps, or cities. One is an earthly city dominated by "love of self to the point of disregard of God." The other is the city of God, which is dominated by "the love of God to the point of disregard of self." In comparing the two, he says "the former glories in itself, and the latter in God" (*City of God* XIV, 28). What we love, he points out, determines who we are.

The people of God live in the city of God. They are not of the world, but live as pilgrims in the world. Their destination is heaven. Their lives revolve around their love of God. Worldly people live in the earthly city. Their focus is on themselves and on material goods and things. They are selfish, self-centered, self-serving, self-aggrandizing, and also unjust.

The Origin of Justice

Justice is defined as fairness and equity. It is one of God's attributes. "The Lord is just" (2 Chronicles 12:6). The love of God compels justice. The people of God, who dwell in Augustine's "city of God," seek that justice. Human justice, a reflection of God's justice, seeks equity and fairness for all humanity.

God's instruction to the people of Israel concerning justice is contained in the book of Deuteronomy: "Do not pervert justice or show partiality. Do not accept a bribe ... Follow justice and justice alone, so that you may live and possess the land the Lord your God is giving you" (16:19–20).

Human justice is opposed by the forces of evil and worldly people motivated by self-love and self-interest. Consequently, human justice is inherently unjust and elusive. Our role as Christians, as citizens of the city of God who live as pilgrims in an unjust and unfair world, is to work for justice, to uphold fairness, and to promote and support issues and causes that seek equity for all the people of the earth.

Equalization of Opportunities

Social justice means the equalization of opportunities and the decrease in the inequities and disparities between the rich and the poor. It is a principle that has been taught since the early days of the nation of Israel when God gave His chosen people the Law. When God's people strayed from social justice, they were warned by the prophets. Isaiah prophesied, "Woe to those who make unjust laws ... to deprive the poor of their rights and withhold justice from the oppressed" (Isaiah 10:1–2).

I want to declare here that it is not acceptable and no longer sustainable for only a few to have plenty while the majority live in need. The current strife and agitation in the world between the haves and have-nots clearly illustrates this point. "True peace is not merely the absence of tension; it is the presence of justice," writes Coretta Scott King in *The Words of Martin Luther King, Jr.* ([New Market Press, 1987], 83). "Blessed are they who maintain justice," says the psalmist (Psalm 106:3).

The goal for the people of God is the elevation and rise of all humanity. Our failure to achieve this goal will mean the eventual fall of all humanity. It is our choice.

Justice as Seen through the Eyes of Dr. Martin Luther King, Jr.

Perhaps one of the most outstanding individuals to represent the cause of justice in our lifetime is Dr. Martin Luther King, Jr. (1929–1968). He looms over twentieth-century American history as a giant who casts a long shadow. In his "Letter from a Birmingham Jail," he explains that human laws are manmade rules that can be either just or unjust (*I Have a Dream: Writings and Speeches That Changed the World*, Harper San Francisco, 1992). Just laws reflect the moral law or the law of God, while unjust laws degrade people rather than uplift them. Men of conscience will uphold just laws and reject unjust laws. Dr. King is categorical on expressing that "injustice can only be uprooted by strong, persistent and determined action" (95).

It is clear that men and women of good will, who delight in the law of God and who love justice and detest injustice, are the only ones who can change the world. Those who are lukewarm and comfortable in an unjust and unfair society, those who uphold the status quo, represent obstacles to progress. Dr. King states that the appalling silence of good people is more damaging to the cause of justice then the evil deeds of the unjust.

Created in the Image of God

The Constitution of our nation, as well as that of many other nations, states that all men are created equal, and they are therefore equal under the law. The Holy Scriptures states that all men are created in the image of God. "God said, 'Let us make man in our image, in our likeness' … in the image of God he created him; male and female He created them. God blessed them and said to them, 'Be fruitful and increase in number'" (Genesis 1:26–28).

God created every human being with distinctive characteristics: some with dark skin, some brown, some white, and others with olive complexion. Some He made tall and strong, others short and weak. Some He created to live by the sea, some to live in the forest and jungles; and others he created to live in the prairies, deserts, and frozen tundra. He gave them all voices with myriads of different tongues, dialects, and languages. They all are the people of the world, His unique creation, each one created equally in His image.

My Story

Although I was born in the United States, I grew up in two different South American countries: Venezuela and Colombia. While I lived there, I was considered a "gringo." Here in my own country, the United States, I am called "Hispanic." In almost every place I have ever been, I have been labeled a "foreigner"—one who does not properly belong or fit, one who is extraneous and out of place.

Without a doubt, of all the countries where I have lived or visited, the place where I received the warmest and most enthusiastic welcome was in Mallorca, Spain. There, for the first time in my life, I was told, "You are from here. You belong here." No words were needed on my part; my surname "Arrom" spoke for me. In Mallorca many people have my surname. My ancestors have lived on that island since the twelfth century, having received land from King Jaime "El Conquistador"

(James "the conqueror") for having helped in the reconquest of the island from the Moors.

José Arrom March, my grandfather, was born in Mallorca in the late nineteenth century. His native tongue was Mallorquín, a language similar to Catalán—one of the four official languages of Spain. He immigrated to Cuba at the end of the nineteenth century when Cuba was still a Spanish colony. My father and my uncles were born in Cuba and eventually came to the United States.

Perhaps due to my life experiences, I consider myself to be a citizen of the world, a man of many lands and many nations. My allegiance and fellowship is with all mankind, with all humanity. In my worldview, all the peoples of the earth are my brothers and my sisters, my mother and father.

My worldview is identical to the teachings of the gospel concerning other people: they all are our brothers and our sisters, and we are to love them as ourselves. In God's family all human beings are His children. No merits or qualifications are needed in order to be accepted. No words are needed; our surname as Christians speaks for us. No one is a foreigner or a stranger. Everyone belongs.

Advocacy for the Poor, the Foreigner, and the Alien

Having lived nearly half of my life in countries of the third world prepared me to be an advocate for the poor, the foreigner, and the alien. In a way, God nurtured me for this role, which explains my strong convictions on the issues of social justice.

Consider, for instance, the case of illegal aliens in the United States. Because they have entered illegally into our country, some feel that is it acceptable for authorities to permanently disrupt them from settling in with their families, to persecute them, to incarcerate them, or even to deport them. God's Word stands in stark contrast. "You are to love those who are aliens, for you yourselves were aliens in Egypt"

(Deuteronomy 10:19). Jesus was Himself an alien in Egypt during His childhood while escaping Herod's persecution. His words stand in contrast as well. His parable of the sheep and the goats says, "Come, you who are blessed by my Father ... I was a stranger and you invited me in" (Matthew 25:34–35).

Every alien person, legal or illegal, is a human being seeking a better life. Every stranger who is persecuted represents Jesus. Jesus says we are to treat them as we would treat Him. "I tell you the truth, whatever you did for one of the least of these brothers of mine, you did for me" (Matthew 25:40). We must let go of our legalism and of our near-sighted economic considerations and see issues as God sees them. In God's economy, all human beings are His children, and He loves them equally. We must do the same.

There is no greater misery then the misery of injustice and ignored suffering. Perhaps because of our own human condition as a fallen race, and because of our own prodigality, as prodigal children of God, the suffering of the world is frequently and conveniently ignored. Justice is also frequently denied.

There is no greater joy than that of justice promoted, of misery and suffering addressed, improved, or resolved. Our human condition is then exalted, reaching to the heavens to touch the hand of God. As in the parable of the prodigal son (see Luke 15:11–32), our Father in heaven rejoices when His lost children repent of their self-righteousness and return home. Humanity's prodigality is then replaced by the commonality of all human beings: what we have in common is far greater than what sets us apart.

To Be Mindful of the Poor

Inevitably we will face the judgment seat of God and be judged on how we responded to the issues of the poor. The gospel of Jesus Christ and the way He showed how His followers are to live require social justice. God Himself chose His Son to be born to a poor family in Palestine. During His life on earth, Jesus lived among the poor and showed us by His example that we are to look after the poor and be mindful of them. Obeying the Law, He told the rich young ruler, was simply not enough. "If you want to be perfect, go, sell your possessions and give to the poor" (Matthew 19:21).

We, as His disciples, are called to help build a better life for all. We are to be concerned not only with our own interests but also to be concerned with the common good. The choice He gave us is this: to walk on our life journey along an egocentric and ethnocentric path that leads to self-destruction, or to give our lives, as Jesus did, for the good of all. The challenges of walking in the way Jesus walked are significant, but the goal is attainable as long as all of us are engaged collectively in this effort.

The words of Nelson Mandela still resonate as clearly today as in 1995 when he said in his speech at the United Nations World Summit for Social Development, "Security for a few is in fact insecurity for all the majority." The present state of affairs in our world where darkness reigns instead of the light of Christ is not acceptable. People should not live and die without ever hearing the name of Christ, as they are doing in many places of this nation and others. Children should no longer die of hunger or of preventable diseases that a one-dollar vaccine could have avoided. Neither can we ignore the suffering of our brothers and sisters in the HIV/AIDS epidemic that is decimating Africa, where the life expectancy in many countries is only thirty-five.

The time is upon us to change the world so that a child born to a poor family in Appalachia or in Africa will have the same opportunities and hopes of a child born into a wealthy family in this country.

The Role of the Church

The church is God's instrument for the transmission of the truth and for the transformation by the gospel of individuals and society.

Social justice is relevant to the mission of the church. It was central in Jesus' message and in His earthly ministry of advocacy for the poor and the oppressed. Likewise, we who are the church and the body of Christ must stand up for social justice. Regrettably, the contemporary church has a disappointing record. It failed to stand for social justice during the Holocaust in Europe and during the times of segregation in the United States.

The church cannot be silent in the face of today's social injustice and the suffering of the poor. If the church is to be true to its calling, it must address the problem of poverty head on. The plight of the poor must be central to our Christian ministry and involve the entire body of Christ. As people are transformed by the gospel, we must change the dynamic of the world of acceptance of the suffering and poverty of the great majority and instead work toward the establishment of a new world order characterized by justice and opportunity for all. As the prophet Isaiah said so well, "Seek justice, encourage the oppressed. Defend the cause of the fatherless, plead the case of the widow" (Isaiah 1:17).

The task may sound overly optimistic, but it is attainable. At the same time, we must not minimize the complexity of the problem. Only the gospel has the power to transform individuals so that we "do not conform any longer to the pattern of this world" but are "transformed" by the renewing of our mind (Romans 12:2). Transformed and empowered individuals can certainly go on to transform society and transform the world.

Many cry, "Yes, we will!" but are not willing to make the necessary changes and sacrifices. The work ahead is worthy of our best efforts, but it is arduous and demands sacrifice. We must face it with faith and courage. We must not be ambiguous about the goal and our commitment to it. We must be resolute and commit.

The day must come when we can look forward with confidence to a tomorrow where our children can all live together in peace and prosperity. Justice is the means to achieve the goal. We must prevail.

A Tale of Two Marys

Several years ago I wrote an article entitled, "A Tale of Two Marys" (previously published in the *Hamilton Journal News*). The article contrasted the very disparate lives of two women, one born in a developed country and the other one born in the third world. It pointed out that their destinies were determined by their place of birth and the services and opportunities that were available to them. It illustrates the brutal reality of life for the world's poor, comparing it with the sheltered and protected life of those born in rich countries. It highlights the unfairness and injustice of the world today while advocating for social justice.

Permit me to introduce you here to Mary of Netherlands and Maria of Mozambique. Mary is a fair and beautiful child born in the Netherlands with a life expectancy at birth of seventy-eight years. Maria is an olive-skinned and also very beautiful girl born in Mozambique, Africa. Her life expectancy at birth is only thirty-seven years.

In the Netherlands, Mary can expect to receive the benefits of vaccinations, have healthy baby visits to a doctor throughout childhood, attend school, receive prenatal care when she becomes pregnant, have safe deliveries for her pregnancies, have health care for the chronic illnesses that she will develop as she ages, live in a safe environment all of her life, and enjoy the provisions of a secure social system.

Maria in Mozambique, on the other hand, will have difficulty in obtaining vaccinations, will probably be malnourished, and will be fortunate to survive beyond the age of five. She will probably not attend school. She will marry young and have five or more children, one or two of whom will die in childhood. She will have no skilled attendants at her deliveries, and with each birth she will risk her own death. She will live in an unsafe environment with poverty and disease, and she will succumb to early death by an illness that would have been prevented or easily treated had she lived elsewhere.

This tale of two Marys illustrates the inequities in health care the world faces today, with a widening gap between developed and developing countries. While on the one hand, one woman has a social support system that allows nearly unlimited expenditure in health care, the other has meager resources that are insufficient and inadequate.

Adequate health care is a matter of social justice that affects us all, raising the question of how to equitably distribute the world's resources so that there is enough for everyone. It is a challenge we must meet.

We are at the crossroads of history. We must take the road of social justice for all or allow the progressive deterioration and degradation of life on planet earth, permitting gaping needs to go unmet and allowing the gap to continue to grow between the rich and the poor, between the haves and the have-nots.

As the gap between the living conditions of Mary of the Netherlands and Maria of Mozambique continues to widen, they both will experience very disparate and almost diametrically different lives. The one's life will be marked by an abundance of resources and opportunities that will allow her to reach her maximum human potential. The other's life will be emblazoned with unmet needs, hunger, and disease, and she will most certainly meet an untimely death.

Here, then, is an appeal for all of us who are the church of Jesus Christ: to seek justice and pursue it. Let us seek fairness and equity for all the peoples of the earth. We must rest in this endeavor because there is great urgency in attaining this goal. The poor of the earth can wait no longer.

In the words of the prophet Amos (Amos 5:24), "Let justice roll on like a river, righteousness like a never-failing stream!"

CHAPTER 20

CHOOSE HAVING A VISION OVER HAVING NO VISION

To have a vision is to have a direction for your life. It is to know your destination and where you want to be in the future. When your vision is intact, you make plans and take steps to conform your life to your vision. You do whatever it takes to achieve your goal.

People with a vision for their lives are purpose-driven people. They waste little time and energy exploring unproductive or unrelated endeavors. They are dedicated to reaching their goal.

A Purpose for Our Lives

Certainly it is beneficial to know as young people what we want to do with our lives. It gives us a clear picture in our minds of how we will spend our time here on the earth. Some know what they want to do sooner than others, but in general the sooner we know the better. We can then focus on achieving our goal and have the satisfaction of a work well done and a mission accomplished.

At some point between the ages of eighteen and twenty-four, most of us embark upon a career or a trade, or we have developed a skill that will allow us to be gainfully employed for the rest of our lives. Others do so more slowly and go longer through life wondering what to do with their lives. For some, our life's work, our vocation, is our vision. For others, our avocation, what we choose to do outside of our work, is our vision.

Being without a vision is like being nearsighted and going through life without the benefit of prescription glasses. Everything is blurry and lacks focus. With glasses, we can see clearly. Similarly, with a vision for our lives we gain focus, and we can discern God's purpose and plan for our lives.

My Vision for My Life

My vision came to me at age seventeen. It was to help others by relieving their pain and their suffering. I thought that of all the ways to serve others, medicine offered the best avenue. I consider myself blessed, because I was given the opportunity to become a medical doctor. The road toward my vision was not without difficulties. It required that I make personal sacrifices and develop discipline in order to achieve my goal.

Of all the things that a person can do for another, relief of suffering seemed the most expedient and the most necessary. And I wanted a rapid, dramatic, and permanent relief for those who suffered. For that reason, as I pursued my vision to become a medical doctor, I chose a surgical specialty—obstetrics and gynecology.

Some may think that surgery inflicts more pain, but this view is incorrect. Surgery's intent is to offer permanent pain relief. Imagine, for instance, a woman suffering from a ruptured tubal pregnancy with massive, life-threatening internal bleeding. Imagine also, by a skillful stroke of the scalpel, the woman's life is spared and the outcome of her suffering is completely changed.

The practice of obstetrics allows me the opportunity to help women navigate through the sometimes dangerous birthing process. It includes looking after both the mother and her yet unborn child during pregnancy. I see myself as being God's humble servant, an instrument in His hands, to help women give birth safely to the next generation.

The gynecology part of my specialty is about relieving pain and healing women from bleeding problems. The story of the bleeding woman in Luke 8 describes how Jesus helped a woman who, I think, was suffering from a gynecological problem. "A woman was there who had been subject to bleeding for twelve years, but no one could heal her. She came up behind him and touched the edge of his cloak, and immediately her bleeding stopped" (verses 43–44).

Seek God First

Determining our vision begins with seeking God. We must first seek His counsel and advice. We must ask Him to reveal His purpose for us. Speaking to Moses, God said, "I have raised you up for this very purpose, that I might show you my power and that my name might be proclaimed in all the earth" (Exodus 9:16).

The Creator made man and His creation for His purpose. He made us for eternity, giving us the Spirit as a guarantee of the promise of eternal life. As stated in 2 Corinthians 5:5, "Now it is God who has made us for this very purpose and who has given us the Spirit as a deposit, guaranteeing what is to come."

The Scriptures also say that God works in us to do His will. Philippians 2:13 states, "For it is God who works in you to will and to act according to his good purpose." Romans 8:28 states, "And we know that in all things God works for the good of those who love him, who have been called according to his purpose."

He created us for a specific purpose and most likely for multiple assignments in fulfilling that purpose. We are uniquely made and qualified to accomplish what He created us to do. Romans 9:21 says, "Does not the potter have the right to make out of the same lump of clay some pottery for noble purposes and some for common use?"

God's primary purpose for us is to live godly lives. He also gave us freedom of choice. The point I have endeavored to make throughout this book is that our choices determine if we fulfill the purpose for which we were created. Those choices also determine whether we enjoy abundant life here on earth and have eternal life with God at the end of our earthly life.

The doctrine of choice is central to the Christian faith. Choice is present for humanity from the very beginning. The book of Genesis states state that God made mankind, male and female, in His image (see Genesis 1:27); but the first man, Adam, chose to disobey God. (The fall of man is related in Genesis chapter 3.)

Like Adam, we have the gift of choice. Our acceptance of God's message of salvation is reflected in our choices. They speak for us; in essence, they show who we really are. Our vision must reflect that we have accepted God's call and are traveling on the right road.

In my opinion, the right road is the road less traveled, the harder one, the one that is not self-seeking but altruistic. Jesus describes finding salvation through Him in similar words. "Enter through the narrow gate. For wide is the gate and broad is the road that leads to destruction, and many enter through it. But small is the gate and narrow the road that leads to life" (Matthew 7:13–14).

Obstacles on our road to achieve our vision are frequent but surmountable. They test, shape, and define our character. Traveling on that road in some parts is like climbing a mountain. The climb becomes steep and difficult, but upon reaching the summit, the view is priceless. From the mountaintop we gain perspective, which allows careful analysis of the panorama and the choice of the correct path to follow as we continue our journey.

To Have a World Vision

Apart from a vision for our lives, having a vision for our community and for the world gives added perspective to God's purpose for our lives. The world's condition is humanity's doing; therefore, it is up to us to change what is wrong with the world.

Just as we have a personal vision, we must have a vision of what the world should be. Do we want fairness and justice for everyone, or just for us? Do we want to share our abundance with others, or just save it for ourselves? Do we want to share our faith with others, or keep it for ourselves as a private matter? Do we simply assume that the most of the world is like us—Christian, well fed, with shelter and equal opportunities—or do we dare to seek the truth? We may be in for a reality shock, for most of the world is not Christian, is poor, is malnourished, lacks shelter, and does not have equal opportunities. And they do not speak English.

Our vision for the world should not be self-serving, but serving of others. It should not be ethnocentric, but inclusive and mindful of others. It should include people of other races, faith, and beliefs with whom we share this planet.

Our vision for the world must include sharing our wealth and abundance with others. We may not consider ourselves rich, but indeed we are. If we think otherwise, our misperception comes from the erroneous comparison with people who have more than we have rather than with those who live on one or two dollars per day, which is the great majority of the world.

Finally, our vision for the world must include the pursuit of things that do not spoil, things of everlasting value, and things that are eternal. Our vision should focus on the kingdom of heaven for all, with all the rights and benefits of citizenship, and also with all the responsibilities. These responsibilities include loving God with all our hearts; loving others as ourselves; sharing the gospel with all peoples; and transforming the world by our love, our works, and the sharing of our God-given resources. Having 20/20 vision is having our lives and the world in which we live in perfect focus.

A Vision of the Coming of the Lord

One day, all of us who have received salvation and have believed in Jesus' name will pass from this life into eternal life. We will live as one with Christ. Our "robes" will be washed white as snow. The final book of the Bible tells us John's vision of this time. "There before me was a great multitude that no one could count, from every nation, tribe, people and language, standing before the throne and in front of the Lamb. They were wearing white robes and were holding palm branches in their hands" (Revelation 7:9).

His vision includes justice for all those who lived without it here on the earth. "Never again will they hunger; never again will they thirst. The sun will not beat upon them, nor any scorching heat. For the Lamb at the center of the throne will be their shepherd; he will lead them to springs of living water. And God will wipe away every tear from their eyes" (Revelation 7:16–17).

This is the final vision: our destination, our resting place. There will be no more suffering and no more tears. And we will live in the house of the Lord forever.

CHAPTER 21

WHAT SHALL I TAKE FOR THE JOURNEY?

Life is a journey. It leads us through familiar and also unfamiliar paths; through what is predictable as well as unpredictable, the planned and the unplanned. Even though we cannot foresee all possible circumstances, we must do our best to plan ahead. At the very least, we must know our destination. We cannot rely on improvisation, for improvisation addresses our current situation but denies us what might have been.

Sometimes events do not unfold as originally planned. Unexpected events require a thoughtful change in course. We must set a new direction that will lead us on a different path. As we pause to analyze the situation, we are confused and bewildered; often we cannot understand the reason for the changed plan. Nevertheless, having accepted God as the ruler of our lives, we know that He is in control of all things. We must therefore trust His plan. Since we are God's people and live as citizens in the city of God, our destination never changes although the path may.

The Grand Plan

Planning for life is like a man going on a journey who carefully studies the route and plans for all foreseeable needs and scenarios. With great attention to detail, he then selects the most useful items for the journey. Similarly, we must also carefully assess potential needs and check them against available resources. Here is a short list of what is most needed for the journey.

1. <u>To have a vision</u>. Nothing compares in life to the efficiency gained by having a vision and knowing our destination. It brings an economy of effort. We set our direction by complete surrender of our will to the Lord. We then ask in faith for His guidance all along the journey.
   Our vision is sometimes revealed to us as a definite vocational calling or mission, with great clarity and unmistakable conviction. Most of the time, it is not revealed to us so dramatically. Instead, it appears as a pathway with open and closed doors.
   Our vision must include changing the world from a place of angst, suffering, and turmoil into a better place. The inequity, injustice, and unfairness in our world pains God and breaks His heart. We are not to be content and accept the status quo, but actively seek change. We are not to rest until change is achieved. God knows that by ourselves we cannot change everything that is wrong with the world, but we can change what has been assigned to us; we can change what we are responsible for, what is our lot and our portion. Everything is possible when God is in it and each of us is diligent in our tasks.
2. <u>To speak the truth</u>. We must stand for the truth; we must be honest to ourselves and to others. We must not speak half-truths or any other form of false statements. We must be zealous in giving authentic and unadulterated truth. "On the contrary, by setting forth the truth plainly we commend ourselves to every man's conscience in the sight of God" (2 Corinthians 4:2).
   In our culture there is an abundance of sound-right sound bites that are only half-truths. Examples: "If it feels good, do it"; "A fetus is not a human being, only a glob of cells"; "I'm okay because I believe in the man up there." We must not accept these false statements as the truth.
3. <u>To choose love as our guide</u>. In all things and in all circumstances, we must look at people and events in the light of God's love.

"Do everything in love" (1 Corinthians 16:14). We must ask: What does God want of us? How does He see us and others? When we see people as God sees them, we gain insight and we have sound judgment. God's love compels us to place others and their needs ahead of ours. Love needs to be front and center in our lives, what guides our thoughts and marks our relationships with the world.

4. <u>To seek wisdom and understanding</u>. We must thirst and hunger for God's wisdom, which is contained in His Word. We must became familiar with it and know it thoroughly. It is our daily, practical source of guidance so that we can know and do what is right in the eyes of God and not what is right in the eyes of the world.

    Wise people seek the counsel of other wise people. In addition to having the Word as our guide, we must listen to the advice of other wise servants of God. Only fools think they know all the answers.

5. <u>To walk in righteousness</u>. Our culture is tolerant and permissive. It allows evil to prosper, as the majority promptly rationalizes it into acceptable behavior. It then becomes the norm and what "everybody does." Some glaring examples of societal permissive behaviors are premarital sex, promiscuity, extramarital affairs, pornography, dishonesty, idolization and glorification of celebrities and athletes, selfishness, and disregard for the poor and for the suffering of the world. We are to reject wickedness. We are to "die to sins and live for righteousness" (1 Peter 2:24).

6. <u>To do what is ours to do</u>. Never assume that others will do what is ours to do. We do not live in the richest country in the world by accident. We have received many privileges, and with them also come responsibilities. Our responsibilities go well beyond our biological family and our church. As responsible citizens of the world, we must transcend the four walls of our church and even our national border, for God expects a lot from us.

As a body of transformed individuals, God expects His church to take a leading role in solving the problems of the world. These problems are our own creation, and it is therefore up to us to fix them. If the church, God's people called to be the light of the world and the salt of the earth, does not act, who will? Who can take our place? We must be like the prophet Isaiah, whose response to God's call is recorded in Isaiah 6:8: "Then I heard the voice of the Lord saying, 'Whom shall I send? And who will go for us?' And I said, 'Here am I. Send me!'"

7. <u>To speak out boldly</u>. Never assume that others will speak for us. As members of the church of Jesus Christ, we must stand up and speak up for the truth, for the poor and the oppressed, for the sick and the dying, for the hungry and the thirsty, and for the alien and the stranger. We must speak for those that have no voice.
8. <u>To believe in ourselves</u>. Never, ever, believe that we cannot be used by God, or that we have nothing to offer. Never believe that we are not good enough or useful enough or knowledgeable enough to serve God. We may only see the overwhelming magnitude of a problem, but God sees the opportunities. He needs only our willingness to be used by Him.

We must not believe the lie that says we cannot be of use to the Master, or that others are better suited or qualified, or that God made a mistake in asking us to do something for Him. God makes no mistakes. He knows exactly what we are capable of doing, and He transforms our meager resources into powerful tools and allows us to accomplish great things in His name.

When Things Do Not Go According to Plan

My second missions trip to the Amazon Jungle of Peru illustrates the point that sometimes unforeseen events force us to change our original plan, and it underlines the importance of trusting in God's plan.

We had planned the missions trip for over a year. We had thought out the details and every possible scenario. We had carefully selected the needed surgical instruments, medication, catheters, sutures, IV tubing, bandages, and more. When the time for departure came near, we packed these supplies into fifty suitcases.

God had chosen every member of the team: twenty-five people from all walks of life. The team was composed of medical and nonmedical people. The medical members of the team included an anesthesiologist, a gynecological surgeon (me), nurses, lab technicians, and a Peruvian dentist. The nonmedical members of the team were from different churches and different cities, having responded to a notice posted in the national Web site of Nazarene Compassionate Ministries.

Three weeks before our departure, the 9/11/01 terrorist attacks upon the United States took place. All flights in and out of the country were grounded. There was widespread uncertainty and distrust of air travel. These circumstances caused the anesthesiologist to withdraw from the team. His decision seemed to be a death blow to a medical mission intent on doing surgery in the jungle. At the last minute, however, we were able to recruit a Peruvian Nazarene anesthesiologist from the city of Chiclayo. This, in and of itself, constituted a great miracle.

It was late in the night when we arrived in Lima, the Peruvian capital. Most of our suitcases were loaded onto a truck, while the team went by bus with a few remaining suitcases. Then terror struck again. The truck with our suitcases and most of our equipment was hijacked at gunpoint as it left the airport. We lost thirty-six out of the fifty suitcases.

A quick inventory of the remaining suitcases confirmed our worst fears. We had lost the majority of our equipment and personal belongings. Most of us had left only the clothes we were wearing. I went to sleep upset and frustrated that night. As team leader, I was responsible for the safety of the team. I had to decide whether it was safe to continue the mission. It was a short night; I slept little.

Early the next morning, the group gathered in the dining room for prayer and breakfast. After prayer, one by one the members of the team rendered their opinion on the significance of the events of the previous day and the course to follow. It was our unanimous decision to go on. We placed our trust in God and accepted His plan, even though it differed from our original plan.

Our mission was very successful despite the loss of the equipment. It was successful not only from the medical standpoint, but most importantly, from the spiritual standpoint. Because of our perseverance in spite of the changes in circumstances, our testimony spoke volumes about our faith, and we gained credibility in the eyes of the people there. God rewarded our decision to carry on.

In the remaining suitcases we still had enough material to handle ten surgical cases at the Nuevo Horizonte mission station. The most difficult surgeries were subsequently done at the regional hospital in the city of Bagua, six hours away from the mission station.

While in Bagua, we established contact with the local Nazarene church. The church people were discouraged because of their inability to complete the construction of their sanctuary. Money had run out, and work had been stopped for several years. In their unfinished temple, we prayed with them for God to provide the means. One year later, a work-and-witness team from the United States helped them finish the project.

We had not planned on being there at all, but God took us there for a reason. Our mission not only touched the lives of the Aguaruna Indian tribe at Nuevo Horizonte, but it also encouraged the church in Bagua.

Similarly, in our lives sometimes things do not go according to plan, and we are set in a different direction. In spite of it, we must not lose sight of our vision, and we must continue to trust in God's plan. While we wrestle with the difficulties of our lives, God already knows the outcome; He is mindful of us, and He has our best interest at heart.

In a Nutshell

What we take for the journey, then, is our vision and our love, seeking God's wisdom and understanding, speaking the truth in the knowledge that we must do what is ours to do to change the world, and speaking out for those who are oppressed—all with confidence that we can be used by God to do great things.

In essence, what we take for the journey is the light, God in us. "Those who know the truth know the light, and those who know the light know eternal life. Love knows the light" (Augustine, *Confessions* VII, 16). God is at the beginning and at the end of the journey. How we travel is our choice.

EPILOGUE

This book was written with you in mind. It was written thinking of what is essential about our Christian faith and of the empowerment of individuals that the good news of the gospel gives. It was written so that ordinary people, like you and me, can find strength and power for our daily lives as well as the motivation necessary to change the world.

This book was written especially for those who are downtrodden and sad, for those who have lost their jobs and their hope in the current economic crisis, and for those who have lost their joy and optimism. It is written in a style that is spiritually uplifting and emphasizes optimism. It intends to shore up spiritual energy and charge up batteries.

Twenty Choices to Abundant Life is not about the gospel of prosperity but about the choices that we make in life. It intends to demonstrate that our faith and the abundant life that it brings have the power to transform not only us but also to transform the world.

It attempts to motivate and inspire the reader to devote his or her best efforts to the service of others and to engage in works that give glory to God. It seeks to encourage the search for the truth that is contained in the gospel of Jesus Christ so that, when our time on earth is done, we can give a good account of our life and be able to hear the voice of the Shepherd saying: "Come, you who are blessed by my Father; take your inheritance, the kingdom prepared for you since the creation of the world. For I was hungry and you gave me something to eat, I was thirsty and you gave me something to drink, I was a stranger and you invited me in, I needed clothes and you clothed me, I was sick and you looked after me, I was in prison and you came to visit me" (Matthew 25:34–36).

ABOUT THE AUTHOR

Robert Arrom, MD, is CEO of The Center for Women's Health and a practicing obstetrician gynecologist in Cincinnati, Ohio. He is a member of the American Medical Association, American College of OB-GYN, and the Christian Medical and Dental Association. He has been a member of the West Chester Church of the Nazarene in West Chester, Ohio, for twenty-two years, serving in the Nazarene Mission International (NMI) Council of his church, and is currently on the Church Board.

Dr. Arrom is a regular contributor to his hometown newspaper, the Hamilton Journal News, as a guest columnist on global and local health issues. He has been a frequent guest, discussing women's health issues, on Cincinnati's WKRC Channel 12 television on a Spanish language program called "Nuestro Rincon." In 2010, Doctor and Mrs. Arrom were recipients of the Barnabas Award, given by the Melanesia Field of the Church of the Nazarene, for their work on advancing the Kingdom of God in Papua New Guinea.

Dr. Arrom's passion is to serve women in their health care needs in his medical practice and in the mission field. He has led six medical missions abroad. He is passionate about the issues of social justice, poverty, hunger, and the diseases of the poor. And he is most passionate about his saving God and being his humble instrument.

With love and respect, the author wishes to donate all royalties from the sale of this book to the Kudjip Nazarene Hospital, located in the Western Highland Province of Papua New Guinea.

This mission hospital of the Church of the Nazarene produces outstanding medical results every day while operating with extremely meager resources. In a country with many deprivations, excellence in medical care is the standard there. Rightfully so, many consider it to be the best in Papua New Guinea, being the only hospital to offer chemotherapy in that country. It represents the best hope and last resort for many of the citizens of the Highlands.

This book is an offering of love to the missionary physicians, nurses, staff, and patients at the Kudjip Nazarene Hospital.

Made in the USA
Charleston, SC
30 April 2011